Personal Organization

**The key to managing your
time _and_ your life**

Personal Organization

The key to managing your time <u>and</u> your life

Harold L. Taylor

Time Management Consultants Inc.
Toronto

3

DEDICATION

To my staff, who help keep me organized.

PERSONAL ORGANIZATION

© 1983, 1988 Harold L. Taylor

Canadian Cataloguing in Publication Data

Taylor, Harold L.
   Personal Organization

ISBN 0-9691407-4-6

1. Time Management. 2. Success
3. Management. I. Time Management Consultants II. Title

HD38.T.39   658.4'093   C83-098484-4

© 1983, 1988 Harold L. Taylor
Harold Taylor Time Consultants Inc.
2175 Sheppard Avenue East, Suite 110
Willowdale, Ontario, M2J 1W8
(416) 491-0777

Printed and bound in Canada
Third printing, March, 1986
Revised paperback edition, January, 1988

TABLE OF CONTENTS

CONCLUSION

Reviewing time management ideas and launching a continuing program of personal organization./**164**

TIME MANAGEMENT
BIBLIOGRAPHY

Other books on the topic of time management and self-management for the more avid reader./**168**

LIST OF EXHIBITS

INTRODUCTION

In my first book, *Making Time Work For You* (General Publishing, 1981), I briefly described how to get organized and summarized effective methods of coping with the various time demands such as meetings, travel, and paperwork. The book also included chapters on delegation and time management in the home. I believe its success was primarily due to the information provided on personal organization, the first significant step to proper time management.

There are dozens of books available which describe time-saving methods of handling telephone calls, visitor interruptions, correspondence, meetings, travel, and so on, but few books go beyond a cursory treatment of personal organization. And yet I have found this to be the most important key to managing time. People, in general, are disorganized. They misplace things, accumulate unnecessary literature, keep inadequate records of telephone calls or visits, work in a cluttered environment, forget assignments and appointments. They have trouble disciplining themselves, getting started in the mornings, handling paper only once, scheduling priority activities and sticking to those schedules. They waste time on trivial items, interrupt themselves and others, work long hours with little to show for it, procrastinate, worry needlessly, set unrealistic deadlines for themselves. And very few of them have set down a set of personal goals, in writing. In short, they are disorganized. And any amount of information on dealing with time robbers will be of little use until people have dealt with the biggest time robber of all — themselves.

Everyone is guilty of disorganization to varying degrees, and there's nothing wrong with a little disorganization in our lives. It prevents us from behaving like robots, adds a little spontaneity to life — sometimes a little comic relief from an arduous job. But when disorganization becomes excessive, it causes wheelspinning, wastes time, and handcuffs our progress. We work harder, put in longer hours, but accomplish less.

This book discusses, in detail, the ways in which disorganization creeps into our lives, and explains how to get back on track. It shows how disorganization on our part not only stifles our own effectiveness, but affects other people as well. It also illustrates how we make ourselves open to interruption by other people. And it shows, step-by-step, how you can organize your work, your environment, and yourself in order to accomplish more in less time. Finally, it explains how to set goals for yourself once the clutter in your life has been banished.

If you have read *Making Time Work For You* but are still dissatisfied about the way you conduct yourself in an office environment, read on. This book is presented almost exactly the way I have presented my time management workshops to thousands of managers throughout the United States and Canada. It assumes you are as disorganized, as I used to be, before

I developed this system of managing myself. If you have not read my previous book, read this one first. Then refer to the other book for additional ideas on coping with those external demands on your time.

Read on. And have the time of your life!

THE CAUSES OF TIME PROBLEMS

The three categories of activities — time wasters, time obligations, and priorities — and the relative importance of each. How to start a program of personal organization.

Chapter One

THE CAUSES OF TIME PROBLEMS

Take a look at Exhibit 1. There's no time problem here, is there? Individual "A" and individual "B" not only have enough time, they have all the time there is to have! We are all the same. We all have twenty-four hours every day for as long as we live. Plenty of time to do the really meaningful things in our lives.

So don't say you don't have enough time. You have 86,400 seconds deposited in your time bank each morning. But how are you spending it? Are you spending it all on priority activities? Well if you are, your day will look something like Exhibit 2. And, as you can see, there is plenty of time for all those priorities in your life. Individuals "A" and "B" are not pressed for time at all. There's plenty of space for priorities such as relaxation, recreation, family and church activities as well as those business-related priorities such as delegation and goal-setting.

What *are* priorities? They are the important, meaningful activities that will lead you closer to your personal and organizational goals. They are the activities that may take only 20 percent of your time, but bring you 80 percent of your results. So it is important to set goals, both in your business *and* in your personal "home" life, in order to have a clear picture of what your priorities really are. But as I mentioned earlier, this is *not* the place to start. You don't have time yet! Let's move on to Exhibit 3 and see *why* we don't have enough time to spend on priorities.

In Exhibit 3 you see a new category of activities added. They are called time obligations. These are the activities that *must* be carried out as a part of your regular day-to-day routine; activities such as talking on the telephone, meeting with someone, travelling to and from work, and writing letters. They may not be priorities, but they *do* contribute, at least indirectly, to your goals. After all, you can't earn a living if you don't commute to work. You can't sell your products without meeting with someone or talking on the telephone. And you can't maintain a household without doing shopping, keeping the house in repair, and washing the dishes.

These are the activities that get the blame for most people's time problems. "How can I get anything done with those infernal telephone calls and drop-in visitors?!" "I'm always being interrupted," or "Those meetings waste most of my day" are common complaints. But although they *do* take time, they are *not* the main problem. If they *were*, you would be unable to control your time at all, because most of the time obligations involve other people. And it's difficult to control other people.

The *real* problem is revealed in Exhibit 4. Here you see the culprits called time wasters, those trivial, time-wasting activities that contribute nothing towards the attainment of your goals. In fact, they could be eliminated and have no detrimental effect on the results you

Exhibit 1

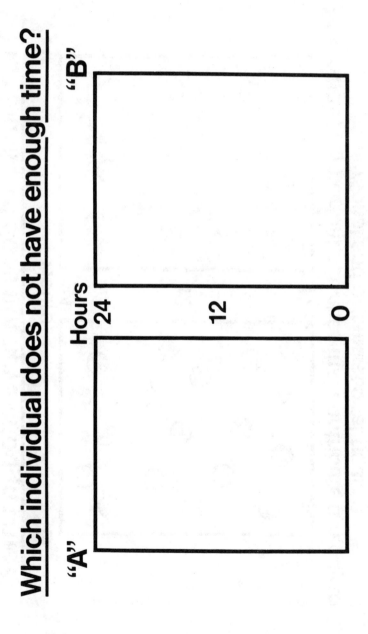

Which individual does not have enough time?

Hours

24

12

0

"A"   "B"

Exhibit 2

Which individual does not have enough time?

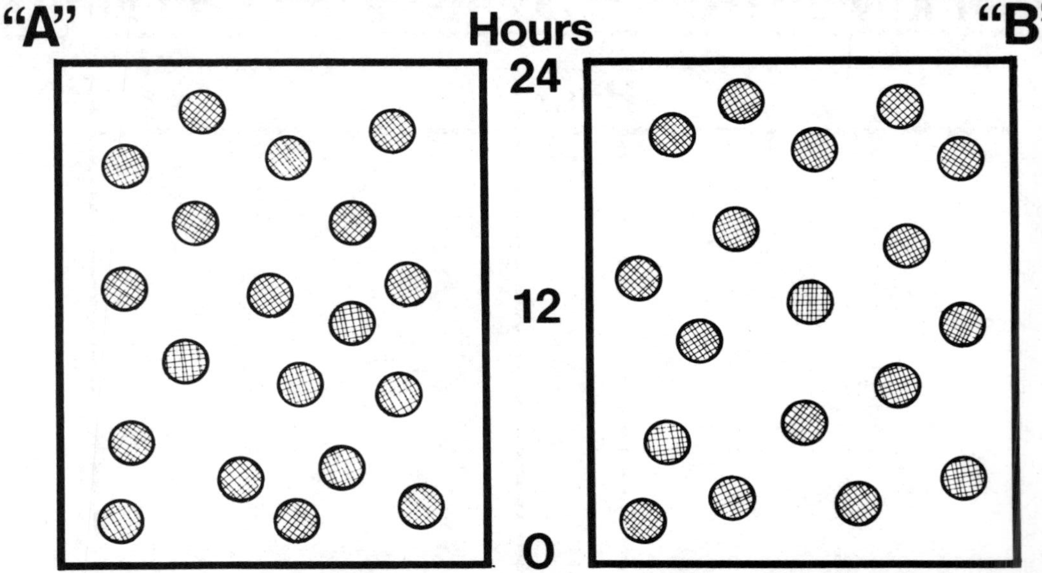

"A"

"B"

Hours: 0   12   24

Priorities: important activities that contribute <u>directly</u> to personal and organizational goals.

18

Exhibit 3

Which individual does not have enough time?

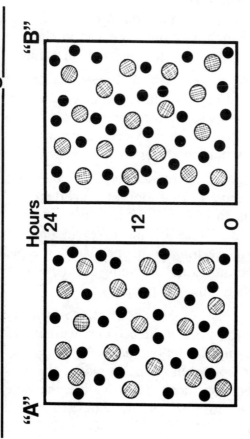

Priorities: important activities that contribute directly to personal and organizational goals.

Time Obligations: less important activities and time obligations that contribute only indirectly to goals.

are obtaining. But if you *could* eliminate them, you would *have* time for those priorities that are now being neglected. The time wasters are those little inefficiencies and bad habits that creep into our lives unnoticed and soon overwhelm us — habits such as procrastination, self-interruptions, and the inability to say no. Inefficiencies that result from a messy desk, a disorganized work area and file system, and the lack of time-saving equipment, forms, and work materials.

Unfortunately, these are the activities that most people ignore (including most time management experts) while they concentrate on the importance of working on priorities. But how can we work on priorities while we are plagued with time wasters.

We haven't got time to delegate, or set goals, or plan, or even relax. Take a look at individual "B" in Exhibit 4. He is so busy coping with the time wasters in his life he doesn't have time to even *think* about delegating, let alone *train* someone. He is the picture of a timestarved individual, jumping from crisis to crisis (since he has no time for planning).

Initially, we must forget about the priorities and concentrate on the time wasters. Once we have eliminated as many time wasters as possible, we swing our attention to the time obligations to reduce the amount of time we spend on them. Then we use the time we save to work on those priority activities, such as delegation, planning, goal setting and self-renewal which will in turn recoup even more time. Our effectiveness will snowball. Once we have some free time it's easier to make ever *more* free time. Time is like money in this respect. It takes money to make money. Give me $100,000 and I'll be a millionaire in no time. But that first $100,000 is hard to come by. Similarly, that first

Exhibit 4

Which individual does not have enough time?

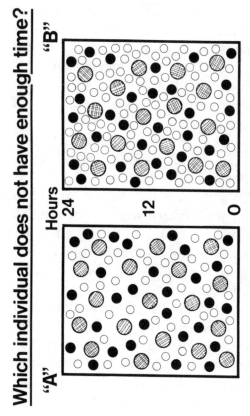

Priorities: important activities that contribute <u>directly</u> to personal and organizational goals.

Time Obligations: less important activities and time obligations that contribute only <u>indirectly</u> to goals.

Time wasters: unimportant and trivial items that contribute <u>nothing</u> to goals.

half-hour of free time each day is hard to come by. It takes time to make time. And the only way we can get it is by winning a minute or two at a time through the elimination of time wasters.

But it's important to use the time we save, the moment we save it. Look at Exhibit 4 again. If we eliminate some of these time wasters, the balance of the activities will simply expand to fill the void. Because activities are like a gas, expanding to fill the container. As an example, suppose you always get up at 7:30 A.M. and leave for work at 8:20 A.M. One morning you wake up earlier and so decide to get up at 7:15 A.M.. Do you leave the house earlier? Probably not. You will dawdle a little longer in the bathroom or spend more time reading the morning newspaper or having a second cup of coffee. The same activities expand to fill the time available for them.

But they won't if you replace that fifteen minutes of sleep you eliminated with fifteen minutes of reading, or writing or some other activity. In fact, with fifteen minutes each day for a year you could probably read the Bible from cover to cover or write a book or mend all your family's clothing or toys.

Similarly, in your business life, by eliminating fifteen minutes of time wasters, you could immediately start spending fifteen minutes each day training your employees to take over part of your job. When they do, you have even more time to invest. Eventually you will be able to spend less time at work and more time with your family. You will have time for exercise, goal-setting, planning, travel, creativity and whatever priorities you have been neglecting because of a lack of time.

Exhibit 5 lists some examples of time wasters, time obligations, and priorities. But remember, *your* prior-

Exhibit 5

ACTIVITIES INCLUDED IN A MANAGER'S LIFE

Time Wasters	Time Obligations	Priorities
Procrastination	Travel	Goal Setting
Forgetting Things	Reading	Planning
Searching for Lost Items	Visitors	Delegation
Shuffling Papers	Boss	Training
Perfectionism	Correspondence	Self-Development
Indecision	Commuting	Creativity
Upward Delegation	Telephone	Self-Renewal
Idle Time	Interruptions	Organizing
Self-Interruptions	Meetings	Family Activities
Inability to say "No"	Crises	
Worry	Mail	
Not Listening		

ities may differ from mine. Once you get organized and have eliminated most of the time wasters and minimized the time spent on the time obligations, you should find some secluded spot in your house or in a park and reflect on what is actually important and meaningful to *you*. There's no sense in saving time if you have nothing meaningful to spend it on. Right now, we have to determine what kinds of time wasters we're plagued with. And then get rid of them.

THE VALUE OF A MINUTE

How time wasters creep into our lives and choke effectiveness. Ways we squander minutes which amount to hours.

Chapter Two

THE VALUE OF A MINUTE

"Look after the pennies, and the dollars will look after themselves." Oh, what a wise old saying! And the same thing applies to time. Look after the minutes, and you have your time problem beat.

We waste minutes shuffling papers, searching for items, forgetting things, interrupting ourselves and others . . . the list of minutes we waste is almost endless. And minutes do add up to hours. If you don't think a minute is significant, how did you get to be as old as you are right now? Life is slipping by a minute at a time, accumulating to form years, and eventually a lifetime. Never underestimate the value of a minute.

Visualize the following scene. You are at your desk and the telephone rings. You interrupt what you're doing and pick up the receiver. "Hello, Oh, Hi Ralph. How are you?" A pause. "Oh, just great thanks ..." The conversation continues, until Ralph makes known the purpose of his call. He asks about a letter he sent to you over two weeks ago that you hadn't gotten around to answering yet. "Oh yes, I have that right here," you reply while searching through the clutter of memos, reports, and folders on your desk. During your search you uncover three or four other items that also require your attention. You pull them into the open, away from the bulk of the clutter — where they can frustrate you and worry you and distract you. You don't have time to *do* them, but you always have time to *worry* about them!

"Yes, I have it," you exclaim as you uncover the object of your search. "What's that? You want me to send 500 folders to you instead of 300? Sure, no problem." Your hand traverses the desk again, this time searching for a scratch pad. In desperation you flip the letter over and scribble notes on the back as he talks. You spot someone coming into your office as you hang up.

"Got a minute?" Sally asks. "Sure," you lie. "What is it?" Then she starts talking about some policy you had rubber stamped and you find out later that she had lied as well, because she ends up taking closer to *twenty* minutes. Of course, that includes three more telephone calls that you accepted while she was in your office. By the time she leaves you have only a vague idea of what she said. By the time you get back to the original report that you had been working on, you have completely forgotten about Ralph wanting the 500 folders. And the notes on his call were buried out of sight on the back of his original letter.

What happens several days later happens several times each week. Ralph calls again. You guessed it; he wants to know where his folders are. You admit that it slipped your mind. Or you blame it on the postal service (which is becoming a more popular ploy). But regardless of what you tell him, here's what you do. You interrupt yourself to see that 500 folders are immediately mailed before you forget again. After all, you let him down and he had to call to remind you, and don't want to go through that embarrassment again! So suddenly, 500 silly little folders command your attention and take precedence over some priority project you may have been working on at the time.

As if interrupting yourself isn't bad enough, you decide to waste your employee's time as well. You call your secretary on the intercom. "Sorry to bother you," you begin, "but could you slip 500 folders into a carton and send them to ..." Did you ever stop to think what your secretary might have been doing when your interruption came? Typing a letter? Talking to a client? In the middle of a telephone call? Whatever it was, it now takes longer to complete and you have succeeded in being somebody else's time waster.

If you only interrupt your employees once each day, that's not bad. But most managers interrupt them continually. As soon as they think of something, they grab for that intercom or telephone (or worse still, interrupt in person) before the thought escapes them. "Oh, Jack, before I forget ..." or "Sorry to bother you again Jan, but I just thought of something else ..." is the usual approach.

Forgetting about the effect on the employees, can you imagine the minutes lost by the *manager* if there are five employees being interrupted four times each in the course of a day?

The scene I just described contains the following time wasters:

> Searching for material
> Forgetting
> Procrastination
> Distractions
> Worry
> Idle time (on the part of an employee)

29

Working on trivial items
Shuffling papers
Not listening

It also contains the following time obligations that could have been completed more efficiently:

Telephone calls
Interruptions
Correspondence
Meetings

There are a lot of minutes to be saved here, minutes that in the course of a few days could add up to hours — hours that could be spent on priority activities that would lead you closer to your personal and organizational goals.

Can you identify with that scene? If so, you should get organized, eliminate the time wasters, reduce the time spent on time obligations, and make room for the priorities.

In the following chapters I'll show you how.

HOW NOT TO GET ORGANIZED

Why most theory doesn't work. The problems with "to do" lists, prioritizing, and starting with time logs.

Chapter Three

HOW NOT TO GET ORGANIZED

In the event that you have already been exposed to the hundred or so odd books and countless seminars on time management, I'd better take a few minutes to explain what *doesn't* work. Everything sounds easy when you read about it, and everything makes sense if you operate in a seminar environment with no telephones ringing or people interrupting you every few minutes. But we are talking about the real world. It's fine for a seminar leader to talk about "quiet hours" as though we could isolate ourselves from the world for hours at a time but, as I exclaim at *my* seminars, "If I bolted my door, they'd come through the windows!" And many of us don't even *have* doors.

I don't know about you, but most seminars and books frustrate me. They tell me *what* I should be doing, but don't really tell me *how* to do it. For instance, I *know* I should delegate, but I can't delegate without taking the time to train my employees, and where do I get the time when I'm already busy from dawn to dusk? The same thing goes for goal setting, planning, creativity, self-renewal and all the other priorities in my life. I just don't have time for these things. That's my problem!

Usually the first thing time management experts tell us to do is make out a time log — a record of exactly how we spend our time over a three or four-week period. If we're behind the gun already, that's all we need — more paperwork.! And the "to do" list! It's a great procrastination tool, since we'd all rather write things down then *do* them. But writing long lists of things to do only succeeded in frustrating me once I saw how many things I actually had to get done — with not enough time to do them. Writing things down rarely results in getting the important things done; it merely encourages us to do the little insignificant things that we can accomplish in a few minutes, just so we can cross off more items and get the list down to a more manageable size. Putting them in order of priority has never prevented this from happening to me because I still have no real commitment to *do* the jobs at a specific time. Not until I started scheduling tasks for a specific time slot in my planning calendar did I succeed in actually getting the jobs done. I'll explain that process later in the book.

The old ABC priority system makes me chuckle every time I think of it. It works. I even described a variation of it in my previous book, *Making Time Work For You*. But it's not practical the way it's taught by the experts, and I've since given it up completely. Let me share my earlier experiences with it.

"Separate all your backlog of paperwork into three piles," the experts told me — "A" priority, "B" priority, and "C" priority. Of course this takes time, since you must read, or at least peruse, each item to determine its importance. And by the time I had all my paperwork separated into three piles, a fourth pile came in! Because everything doesn't conveniently come in to a standstill while I'm doing my sorting. Then I was told to force myself to make a decision on the "B" priority pile — either put the items in the "A" pile or in the "C" pile. Now tell me, why did they encourage indecision by having this middle pile in the first place? It's a waste of time! Then they have the nerve to come up with the principle "handle each piece of paper only once" in the same book. As if this isn't bad enough, the next step is to put the "A" priority pile in some obvious spot (a top drawer or on the top of the desk) and the "C" pile in a bottom drawer. Does anybody in my state of disarray actually have two empty drawers?

Although I make fun of the method, the intention is sound. The experts want us to start on that priority pile and work on it first, one piece at a time. Unfortunately, even if we survive the sorting period, most of us do not have the self-discipline to work on that pile very long amid all the enticing distractions of an office environment.

In fact, the problem with most time management authors and seminar leaders is that they assume we will quickly acquire the necessary discipline by some power of positive thinking. In reality, this isn't so. One of the reasons that managing our time is so difficult is the fact that it depends so heavily on self-discipline. That's why I had to resort to organized forms and systems that forced me into a specific routine. Over a period of time I formed good time management habits and gradually broke most of the time wasting habits that I had developed during my lifetime. *You can do the same* — not by some sweeping "overnight" changes involving delegation, time logs, and "to do" lists, but by a gradual change in your working habits aided by tools such as a proper planning calendar and "Personal Organizer" (to be described later).

Finally, you must rid yourself of the notion that your time problems are caused by other people. Books and seminars tend to suggest this by the amount of time they devote to interruptions, telephone calls, visits, formal meetings and other external problem areas. The main reason for your time problem is *you*, not other people.

I found this hard to accept. I spent years blaming other people, rationalizing my own inefficiencies. There was a time when I seldom took holidays, worked weekends, put in late nights. And I claimed it was necessary because of the nature of my position. It took a major shake-up in my life, including a case of bleeding ulcers, to make me realize that *I* was the problem. And that only *I* could solve it. Well, I solved it, but it took more than seminars and books. It took a willingness to admit that I was the one being described in the previous chapter. And that I had to clean up my own act first, before turning my attention to others.

CLEAN UP YOUR ACT

The initial clean up. How to use a planning diary to schedule tasks before your time is monopolized by people. How to protect that time.

Chapter Four

CLEAN UP YOUR ACT

The only time some people have a clean desk is when they're expecting an important visitor. They quickly gather up all the paperwork, reports, and magazines that are strewn about and stash them on an over-burdened shelf, or out of sight. When the visitor leaves, they re-sort it to find the various items they were working on. If they have several important visitors each day, they spend more time burying and retrieving materials than they do working on them.

I know what it's like to work with a messy desk. The only time my employees could find a clean spot to place a typed letter was when I was out of the office. They could place it on my chair! No one dared use the in-basket — the letter may not be seen for a week. Amazing how we call them "in-baskets" when they're used as "holding-baskets". Anything we haven't got time to do — or don't like to do — gets thrown back into the in-basket. What's the date on the oldest piece of correspondence in your in-basket? If it's only a few days old, that's unusual. We could probably date a manager in terms of how long he or she has been on the job, simply by digging into the in-basket. Peeling back layer after layer, we would reach letters and memos which date back to job orientation time or even the original employment date!

The in-basket should be emptied daily. Schedule at least twenty minutes or a half-hour each day to go through your mail. But first, clear off that desk. A desk is a work surface, not a storage area. So treat it that way. Forget about sorting into priorities. Arrive at the office early (or use an evening or a Saturday) and toss everything into one big pile. If it falls over, use *two* piles and *two* Saturdays. Scrap everything that's unimportant. If in doubt, throw it out. During the initial clean-up period you may have to toss out all junk mail, magazines, form letters and newspapers unread. Until the desk is clear we're only interested in the 20 percent of the materials which represents 80 percent of the value. Complete all the work you can. Boil the pile down to a minimum. What will be left are those important reports, projects and letters that will take over a half-hour to complete. You don't have a half-hour, or *ten* hours to do them now. So what you do is *schedule a time to do them.*

Don't put them on a "to do" list! Take out your planning diary, preferably a week at a glance, with times marked off in fifteen minute or half-hour increments, and block off a definite period of time in which to complete those tasks. Do it now, before your planning diary becomes filled with people.

Most managers fail to use their planning diaries to schedule tasks. They simply use them as calendars and record meetings and appointments. No wonder there's no time to complete long projects. The better part of their day is consumed by people.

I was no different. At one time if anyone had asked how my week went, I needed only to refer them to my planning diary. It was filled with scribbled-in names of people and places. I was forever jumping from one appointment to the next. If they had asked me how *next* week was going to be, I couldn't have told them. At least, not by the looks of my calendar! It was practically empty. I knew I would be busy. But I didn't know at what. I operated like Horatio Alger — "Come and get me." And they did. Interruption after interruption.

Every time someone wanted to see me I would oblige. After all, my calendar was empty — at the disposal of anyone who wanted my time. "Harold, could I see you at 9:30 A.M. tomorrow?"

"Sure, Sally, that would be fine," I'd reply. In fact it was a *great* time, because it broke up the morning — the time that I was at my productive best. I wouldn't dare ask her how long the meeting would take; that would be impertinent! And I certainly wouldn't ask her what it was about. After all, we all appreciate that element of surprise! And if Bill phoned and wanted to see me as well, I'd tell him not to come in until 11:00 A.M. just to be on the safe side. After all, Sally may need a little extra time. And if Sally's meeting didn't drag out, perhaps I could even work on something important for five or ten minutes.

John calls. "Are you busy tomorrow afternoon?" "No", I promptly reply. After all, how could I be busy, I had no *people* scheduled there yet. Think for a minute. If my boss called and asked if I would be busy tomorrow and I answered "no," he should fire me! Why do we define "busy" as having people with us? In actual fact, we are busier *and more productive,* when there are *no* people with us.

Tom calls. Then Susan. My planning diary gets filled with *people,* with plenty of spaces in between. Within those spaces, between interruptions, telephone calls, and crises, I try to get my priority work done. No wonder I was spinning my wheels and working overtime. I had my priorities mixed!

Don't mix up *your* priorities. Schedule those important tasks — those jobs that you were hired to accomplish — *before* your calendar gets filled up with people.

You cannot work effectively in scattered fragments of time. Consolidate those fragments to form a half-hour, hour, or more, and block it out on your planning calendar as illustrated in Exhibit 6. In the space, jot down a word or two to identify the task you have committed yourself to complete at that time. If you have a ten hour job to do, you probably cannot block out more than two hours to work on it at any one time. But schedule five of those blocks over the next few weeks. Plan it so you'll complete the project well in advance of the deadline. Most of the "unrealistic" deadlines we encounter are caused by our failure to schedule the task immediately upon being aware of it. The "do it now" or "start it now" habits are essential if you are going to gain control of your time. Isn't it odd that the panic, frustration, and stress we experience as we race towards a deadline involves a job that we knew about weeks or months ago? Our tendency to procrastinate, combined with our inability to say "no" to those daily "people" demands, keeps us disorganized and harried.

Well, the above procedure will help you to overcome this universal problem. Unlike a "to do" list (which produces no real commitment), the practice of actually blocking out a definite time to perform the task produces an obligation to *act*. It's there in black and white, like you would schedule a meeting. And you will have protected that time from the demands of oth-

Exhibit 6

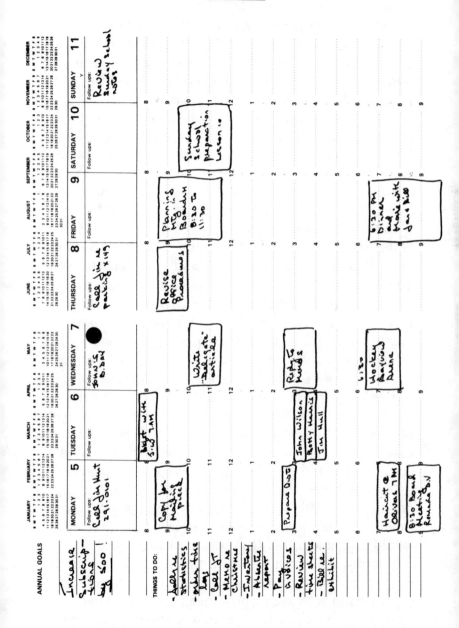

43

ers. For instance, when Sally phones and asks if you're busy at 9 A.M. on Tuesday, you can actually answer "yes" in all honesty. And not feel guilty about it! Don't ever feel you need to apologize for working on a priority job — one that you were hired to perform, and that will help the organization reach its goals.

You will be amazed how flexible other people can be. If you're tied up at 9:00 A.M., Sally will probably come up with a second choice. But don't even wait for her to do that. *Suggest a time yourself.* Telling a person "anytime after 10:00" is opening your calendar to others. Don't give people free access to your time. Your time is your most valuable resource; don't treat it as though it were worthless. If your "project time" is due to end at 10:00 A.M., suggest 10:00 A.M. But not until you've asked what she wants to talk to you about. After all, you might be able to settle the matter right then on the phone and save the time of a meeting. If you decide to see her, don't waste time talking about the problem on the phone — you'll cover the same things again when you meet.

And don't be afraid to set a time limit. A simple "How long do you think it will take us?" will suffice. If she replies, "Oh, it will only take us about five minutes," tell her you'll block off fifteen "just in case." Your actual words might be "Well, I don't want us to run out of time, Sally. What say I block off fifteen minutes? I won't schedule any other appointments until 10:15." Always give people more time than they ask for, which is less time than they would take, and usually the exact time they need.

You schedule start and stop times for formal meetings, so do the same with appointments. Make sure the other person is aware of how much time they have. All activities expand to fill the time available for them, and meetings and appointments are no exception. If you allow a half an hour, it will *take* a half an hour.

Try to stack appointments to ensure that they don't run overtime. If the next person asks to see you at 10:30 A.M., ask, "Can you make it at 10:15? I'll be free then." This makes it important to end the *first* meeting by 10:15. After all, you don't want to keep someone waiting! So you have a "legitimate" reason for concluding the business promptly.

Don't tell your secretary to lie for you by calling you on the intercom to rescue you from the meeting. Imaginary appointments and "make-believe" emergencies do nothing for your credibility. I suggested a few similar deceptive tactics in my earlier book *Making Time Work For You,* and I regret it. In my enthusiasm to save time I carried things a little too far. If you follow the advice in this book it isn't necessary to be dishonest.

HOW TO KEEP YOUR DESK CLEAN

How to use a follow-up file to keep projects off your desk. Organizing your work area.

Chapter Five

HOW TO KEEP YOUR DESK CLEAN

I'll provide more suggestions as to how to protect the time you have scheduled for those priority projects in the next chapter. But right now, you have a handful of material relating to that project and nowhere to put it. And you certainly can't leave it on your desk or toss it back into the in-basket. So what you need is a follow-up file as shown in Exhibit 7.

This follow-up file is exclusive of your secretary's. If your secretary keeps a follow-up file and uses it to jog your memory or return letters, reports, etc. to you for follow-up or approval, that's great. But this is *your* personal follow-up file which contains the back-up material for those tasks that you have scheduled in your planning diary. Nothing goes into this follow-up file unless a time to complete it has been blocked off in your planning diary.

The follow-up file system consists of thirteen hanging files marked January, February, etc., and the last one marked "next year." One set of manilla folders marked from 1 to 31, corresponding to the days of the month is placed in the current month's hanging folder.

Exhibit 7

"Follow-up" File System

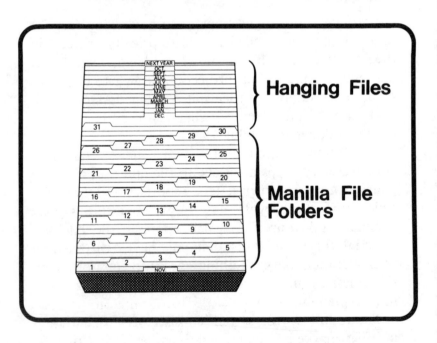

Hanging Files

Manilla File Folders

If it's the first of the month and you have emptied the day's project papers, move the manilla folder to the next month's hanging folder. You will be able to schedule tasks up to 31 days in advance, keeping the relevant papers in the folder which corresponds with that date.

This follow-up file system is simply an adjunct to your planning diary. Your diary contains your work plan. When you arrive in the morning, flip open your planning diary and see a report scheduled for 9:00 A.M., you know exactly where to look for the back-up papers needed.

If *more* papers are received related to a specific task that is scheduled for a future date, it's a simple matter to find the appropriate follow-up file folder. Simply flip through your planning diary to find the date on which that project is scheduled.

For on-going projects such as committee meetings, book manuscripts, and bulky engineering projects, it's not necessary (or advisable) to jam all the back-up material into the follow-up folders. Instead, use a coloured manilla folder bearing the project's name or title. Keep them in your right hand desk drawer, along with your follow-up file. Use hanging folders for these project files for easy retrieval. You will soon know that the red folder is "A" project, the green folder "B" project, and so on.

Once you have cleared your desk, and scheduled the jobs you didn't have time to do right away, you're well on your way to being organized. A few hours invested in this initial clean-up will save millions of precious minutes in the future. You will have eliminated some time wasters — shuffling papers, searching for things, distractions, working on trivial items. While you've got the momentum, do a good job of this initial clean up. Empty those desk drawers, that shelf under your desk, those cluttered bookcases, credenza and filing cabinets.

Muster up enough courage to throw out anything you can't see an immediate use for. Have a place for everything and put everything in its place, within reason. But leave yourself the luxury of one junk drawer for all those U.F.O.'s (Unidentified Funny Objects) you have collected such as gold plated paperclips, unusual business cards, and your son's handcarved thumbtack holder. You can carry the organization bit a little too far.

No executive or homemaker can do without that single junk drawer. We all need a *little* disorganization somewhere in our lives. And sorting through that junk drawer every six months or so is more fun and more stress-relieving than an executive sandbox.

Once you have cleared your desk and emptied your in-basket, don't dump things back in again. People are tempted to use it as a holding basket for everything pending or puzzling. Don't. The trivial items will obscure the important ones, which soon become urgent. Fight procrastination by looking at it as an *action* basket.

Once you have emptied your in-basket, don't leave material on your desk. Scrap it, delegate it, complete it, or put it in your follow-up file for future action.

You'll be tempted to leave material on your desk temporarily, until you have a chance to work on it. Don't. You'll soon have so much temporary storage, it will become permanent clutter. You'll waste time searching for items. The minutes add up to hours. All those unfinished tasks scattered before you will produce anxiety and stress. You'll be tempted to hop from one unfinished job to another. You'll have difficulty concentrating on the task at hand. Messy desks decrease effectiveness. After all, who can plan with all those urgent, unfinished tasks taunting them?

A clear desk will give you a psychological lift. You'll look organized, you'll feel organized, and you *will* be organized.

ORGANIZING YOUR OFFICE

Arranging your office furniture to minimize interruptions. Organizing the office area to decrease time waste.

Chapter Six

ORGANIZING YOUR OFFICE

Make sure your private office is arranged so as to attract a minimum of interruptions. Don't face the open doorway. Have your desk to one side, so people will have to go out of their way to see you. Or have your desk facing away from the doorway. If they are able to catch your eye from outside the office they will be tempted to walk inside and strike up a conversation. For the same reason, avoid having gathering spots outside your office such as coffee or photocopying facilities. One manager reported that the coffee maker was right outside his office door and people would kill time while the water boiled by walking into his office and socializing.

Although the absence of chairs would make unscheduled visitations brief, it would also make *scheduled* meetings inconvenient. But don't have chairs close to your desk or facing you unless you're short of room. They're an open invitation for people to slip into them. Instead, place them about six feet or more from the desk, and have them *facing each other*. The awkwardness of sitting that far away and looking at you over their shoulder should discourage anyone from heading for the chairs. When the drop-in approaches your desk, you can stand, and remain standing until the brief conversation is over. If you want to carry on a lengthy conversation, simply move from your desk to the chairs and carry on the conversation in the open, facing each other, without the barrier of a desk between you.

Have your office decorated tastefully, but simply. A lot of family photos, trophies, certificates, and citations will encourage chit chat. Don't have ashtrays if you don't smoke. Or comfortable sofas if you don't sleep in your office. But plants are great, even if you don't garden. And a clock is a great reminder of the speed at which time passes; place it where your *visitor* can see it.

Arrange your working tools and furniture closely around your desk area. Don't place frequently used filing cabinets or bookcases on the other side of the room. You should have everything at your fingertips. Have an adequate inventory of felt pens, paperclips, staples, highlighter markers, etc. in one of your desk drawers. Don't skimp on office supplies; have your own stapler, three-hole punch, self-inking stamps. Sharing with other people is *not* economical when you take lost time into consideration.

Your desk does not have to be large but you must have sufficient working area. The desk is not meant for storage, so keep it clear of paperwork except for projects you are working on. Other projects should be retained in a follow-up file; the bulkier ones can be kept in colored manilla folders, clearly identified. These should be kept in hanging files in your desk drawer. If your desk doesn't have a drawer large enough to hold files, I recommend you get one that does. If this is impossible, keep the follow-up file system and project files in a vertical file holder on the top of your desk or in a filing cabinet to the side of your desk.

Keep articles, procedures, job descriptions, policies, product bulletins and anything else that you refer to frequently in three-ring binders. Label them clearly for easy identification; buy some self-adhesive insert holders for the spines of these binders. The bookcase or shelf should be within reach. Surround yourself on three sides with your working materials.

Your office should be arranged so that everything is readily accessible. Every time you have to walk to the main office for supplies, you risk an extended interruption. So anticipate the envelopes, letterhead, pads, etc. that you will need, and include them in your inventory. If you need an extra cabinet or shelf on the wall near your desk, get one. Have a set of stacking trays on your desk or credenza bearing the names of the people who report to you, or who you communicate with on a regular basis. This could include your boss. Whenever there is something requiring their attention, jot notes on it and toss it in one of those trays. Invariably, they will interrupt you at least once every day and they can empty their tray when they do. Don't deliver mail to anyone who will be dropping in. Save yourself some trips.

Don't let your office environment control you. You spend too many hours there to suffer unnecessary inconveniences. If a floor receptacle prevents you from placing your desk where you want it, have the outlet moved. If the door is in the wrong place, change it. If the lighting is poor, add more lights. If the rollers on your chair are worn, replace them. Any costs incurred are one-time costs; the time savings are forever. Experiment with several arrangements until you get the

Exhibit 8

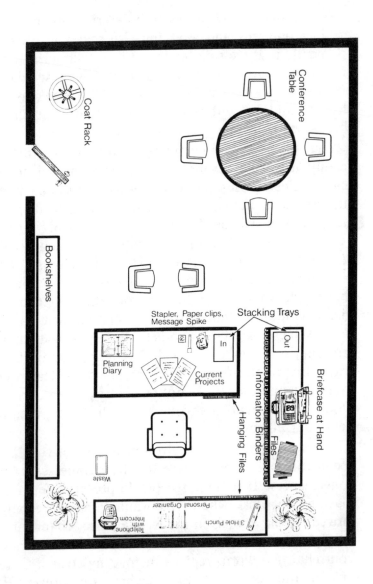

Sample Office Layout

56

one that works best for you. Exhibit 8 shows the arrangement of my office at the present time. It differs from the way it appeared in *Making Time Work For You*. I discovered couches were too comfortable and encouraged socializing, but chairs placed around a conference table encourage results. I moved the telephone so I would have my back to the door when using it. This removed the temptation to be distracted by anyone walking into my office. You can't pay attention to two people at the same time.

If you don't **have** an office, do what you can to build privacy into your "territory." Use dividers, bookcases, plants, and filing cabinets to shield yourself from eye contact with other people. Locate your desk away from the main thoroughfare of traffic is possible. Researchers have concluded that privacy encourages job satisfaction and increases performance.

If you can influence the layout of the main office, do so. Place office equipment so as to minimize steps while keeping in mind the possible distractions. Decentralize storage cabinets so everyone's supplies are close at hand. If you need a centralized storage room, make sure it's easy to locate the various supplies. Try painting the shelves in the supply cupboard different colors. All stationery, letterhead, forms and paper products could be kept on the green shelf, all typewriter and other office equipment supplies on the red shelf, all small office supplies such as paperclips, rubber bands, staples, etc. on the blue shelf — and so on. Everyone would soon get to know they could find the timesheets on the green shelf and the correction fluid on the red shelf, and it would make it easier to tell new employees and visitors where to find something.

Tape a copy of the form, folder, envelope, etc. to the outside of each carton to identify the contents. A few minutes spent identifying and storing the materials properly will save hours later.

HOW TO HANDLE YOUR MORNING MAIL

Scheduling mail time. How to dispense with routine paperwork quickly. Acquiring the "do it now" habit and avoiding mail delivery distractions.

Chapter Seven

HOW TO HANDLE YOUR MORNING MAIL

Most people catch "clean up" fever every so often and spend a weekend or more cleaning their desk and getting rid of their backlog of work. But the clean-up portion of their efforts goes for naught. They have not invested time, they have wasted time, because in a week or more they're right back where they started, messy desk and all.

To prevent this from happening to you, develop a system of handling all incoming material to dispose of it or schedule a time to do it later. To me, the morning mail used to be an interruption. No matter how important a job I was working on at the time, I used to pounce on that mail the moment the secretary disappeared. (It's interesting to note that I did not pounce on it in the secretary's presence. I would maintain my composure and curb my "Type A" tendencies until she was out of sight. *Then* I would be my normal impulsive, inefficient self.) I never really got much accomplished when I sorted through the mail. After all, I didn't have the time right then; I was *busy* working on an important project. Yet I would make time to sort and shuffle and rearrange and sometimes even make the odd phone call as a result of a letter or memo I had received. I always managed to get sidetracked for five or ten minutes before picking up where I had left off on that important project. Unfortunately, I could never really pick up where I left off without first backtracking and reviewing and getting reoriented to the task. Mail-time was interruption-time for Harold Taylor.

But no more. Now I schedule a time for it, and ignore it until that time arrives. If you don't think your willpower is strong enough to do this, move your in-basket outside your office so you won't be tempted.

The secret of handling mail is to "handle" it as little as possible, and to get rid of it quickly. If someone else opens your mail and screens it, most of it need never reach you. Have it diverted to your subordinates and let *them* handle it. They can keep you posted by sending you a photocopy of their reply — which you can promptly scrap. The real important items will reach you via your subordinates, along with their input, so you can handle it quickly.

If you insist on seeing all of it, don't allow it to accumulate. Use that time that you have scheduled and dispense with *all* of it. When someone else opens your mail for you, make sure they separate it into priority, routine and junk mail. Have them put the priority items into a red manilla folder, the routine items in a yellow one, the junk mail in a blue one (or pick your favourite colors). The mail should come to you in that order — the red folder on top, the blue folder on the bottom, followed by any magazines.

Start with that top folder and work on it. These are the items which will bring you 80 percent of your results. Do what you can, and schedule the rest using your follow-up file to house the material. Resist the urge to shuffle through the other folders looking for quick and easy tasks. And don't waste your time on interesting but useless literature that should be relegated to your "junk mail" folder.

If you never get to the "routine" or "junk mail" folders, you haven't missed much. Give them back to your secretary and he or she can add to them the next day.

When you schedule a time each day to work on your mail, it could be fifteen minutes or half an hour, depending on your experiences. Use that time to get rid of the paperwork. If you simply sort through it and set it aside, you'll be buried in no time.

Here's how you can dispense with the various items quickly. These are representative of the categories of paperwork that most of us receive daily.

Meeting notices

Record all the pertinent information such as time, place, topic, in your planning diary and *scrap* the notice. Have a planning diary that's portable and keep it with you wherever you go.

Trivial letters

These are the ones requiring no reply. Note and scrap. Resist the urge to write back if a reply would accomplish nothing. And don't file them.

Important letters

Reply immediately, preferably by phone. If it has to be in writing, dictate a reply using a cassette recorder. If informality is in order, write your reply directly on the letter or use a speedimemo. Don't procrastinate.

Lengthy letters or projects that are important

If it's going to take you over twenty minutes to formulate a reply, write a report, or collect information, schedule it for later. But commit yourself by recording the task in a specific time slot in your planning calendar. Place the back-up material in your follow-up file under the corresponding date.

Magazines

Don't toss them aside. Check the index and rip out or photocopy any articles that look worthwhile. Staple and three-hole punch them and toss them into your briefcase for reading during idle time. Scrap the magazine itself. If it's to be circulated, *photocopy* the article instead. After reading, file the articles in three-ring binders, a separate binder for each topic.

Junk mail

Most people get good ideas or information from this unsolicited material, so take the time to leaf through it. Make notes on anything of interest *which you plan to act on* and slip it into an "idea" file. Check this "idea" file once per week and either put your ideas into practice, schedule a time to do it, or scrap the material. Don't allow it to accumulate. Any idea, no matter how valuable, becomes useless if not put into practice.

Minor requests

These can probably be handled quickly during the time allotted for your mail. If not, jot them down in your planning diary — not in any particular time slot, but on the left hand side in the "things to do" column. (Refer back to Exhibit 6).

Most of those urgent tasks that keep us working under stress and burning the midnight oil were *not* urgent at one time. They were simply part of the paperwork that arrived in the mail and kept getting tossed back into our in-basket or allowed to remain among the clutter on our desk. That is the reason it's so important to work on your incoming mail every day, disposing with the items or scheduling a time to do them.

An important project will never become an urgent one if you use this method. We have enough legitimate crises occurring without manufacturing some of our own. Don't follow the advice of some time management experts who tell us to allow an "aging period" on all requests on the chance they'll die a natural death. How would you like *your* requests to be ignored. Give prompt replies. If you delay replying to letters, you not only waste time, you antagonize the writers. You're really telling them, "I don't care enough about you to suffer the inconvenience of answering your letter. I'm too busy to be bothered." And everyone knows we're never too busy to do the things we really *want* to do.

If the letter doesn't call for a reply, don't give one. But if it requires a response, a telephone call or a scribbled note on their letter or speedimemo is far better than the selfish "ignore all memos" approach. A prompt reply will not only save time by eliminating follow-ups and keeping a clutter-free desk, it will maintain friendships. The "do it now" habit is a must if you want to manage your time effectively. For the tendency to procrastinate increases each time you put something off.

So what if you *do* comply with a few trivial requests that you could have ignored without the boss being the wiser? What's wrong with having a reputation for being prompt, efficient, cooperative, and organized? It's a lot better than managing by crises, being under pressure, harried, disorganized, and unable to meet deadlines.

Since the bulk of the requests, assignments, and projects arrive via the mail, make sure you keep on top of it. This involves spending as little time as possible in getting the job done. Before writing a letter, ask yourself if it's necessary. Don't write a letter just to tell somebody what you're planning to do, or to thank them for a thank you letter.

Don't write letters longhand if they're going to be typed afterwards. Use a cassette recorder. There are some good models available. You can dictate while you drive, walk or wait for someone. And with practice you will be able to dictate brief, crisp letters without all the "fill" that wastes *everybody's* time.

Jotting a brief message on your business card and clipping it to the material requested is a real time saver — and provides a personal touch. Trouble is, most business cards don't allow any room to write on. Try adding a perforated section to the card (blank except for the word "message"). The perforated "message" can be tossed away and the business card retained. It's also very handy when your new acquaintances are "out of cards." Simply tear off the "message" part and have them write their name and phone number on it, then give them the business card portion to keep.

Another time saver is the "post it" notes from the 3M Company. These yellow mini-scratch pads come with a strip of pressure sensitive glue along one side and are a real time saver with multiple uses. Just peel them off and slap them on a book, magazine, letter, report — anything you want to pass on to someone or circulate. Jot down your personal message or instructions. The "post it" notes can be easily peeled off and discarded later.

Since the purpose of this book is to supplement my first book, not to replace it, I will not repeat the suggestions contained in *Making Time Work For You*. But I do recommend you read Chapter 6, "Control The Information Explosion" and Chapter 9, "Slay the Paperwork Dragon" in that book for full coverage on correspondence and paperwork.

I will offer one further suggestion not mentioned in my previous book. If you want to keep certain reference magazines "intact" have them bound in hard cover. You can have between twenty-four and thirty-six issues (depending on the magazine's thickness) bound in one "volume," with the title and dates on the spine for easy identification on a bookshelf. Have different colored bindings for different magazines. No more searching through stacks of magazines or shelves. No more "missing issues." No dog-eared pages or torn magazines. A real timesaver. Only for good reference magazines though — ones you would keep on your shelf in your library.

The cost is about $15 to $20 per volume. Call a local bindery for quotes.

THE VALUE OF A QUIET HOUR

How interruption-free segments of time can multiply your effectiveness.

Chapter Eight

THE VALUE OF A "QUIET HOUR"

I hesitate to use the term "quiet hour" since no hour is entirely "quiet," at work *or* at home. But it's the accepted term, and refers to the attempt to maintain that block of time that you have set aside for a specific task relatively free of interruptions. You won't eliminate *all* interruptions, and for that reason I recommend you schedule up to 50 percent more time than you think you will need to complete a job. But you will be able to eliminate *most* interruptions once you make up your mind that you deserve as much respect as anyone else.

I say this, because many people feel it's unethical to have calls and visitors intercepted when there's no one in their office with them.

There's nothing unethical about closing your door and having a "meeting with yourself" so you can spend some undisturbed time on priority tasks. But some people feel guilty. They think they're deceiving their fellow employees by suggesting they are with someone, when in actual fact they are alone. And no wonder. Some people go to great lengths to convince other people that they are involved in something else.

I've heard of one person who tells his secretary he's going out on consultation, when "Consultation" is the name of a boat he owns. Another leaves word that he's on course, when it's actually a golf course.

When you get to the point of having to deceive others into thinking you're doing something other than spending quiet time alone, the quiet time will not be effective; too much time will be spent in the deception, and not enough in the individual attention to the task at hand.

It's a fact of life. People are more productive when they can work at something undisturbed. At least one hour each day spent in seclusion, away from ringing telephones and drop-in visitors, is the sign of an effective manager. So make it part of your daily routine, but don't overdo it. If your door is always closed people will ignore it and walk in anyway. And make sure people know how long you will be tied up. A word to your secretary, or a sign on the door, "Available at 3 P.M.", is sufficient.

And above all, don't feel guilty that you're making yourself unavailable to employees, peers, outsiders, and your boss for that period of time. If you're interrupted in what you're doing for only one minute, it will take another three minutes to recover. A "quiet hour," where no interruptions are allowed except emergencies, will magnify your effectiveness. Fight for it. If people ignore your closed door, post a sign on it. If your boss or employees object, show them the *results* of that quiet hour. There *will* be results. Those people who have gotten up early and worked for an hour at the kitchen table will realize this. You can get about three times as much accomplished when interruptions are completely eliminated. This assumes you don't interrupt *yourself*. The temptation to do this is great. Because we're used to being interrupted so much we miss it when it doesn't happen. Discipline yourself. Just once, make up your mind to work at a project for a whole hour without stopping to take a walk, a stretch, a coffee or to daydream or stare out the window. The results of that hour will be your reward, and your incentive to do it again the next day. And though it may be painful, one hour of steady work is definitely not injurious to your health.

Don't lose sight of the *reason* for a "quiet hour"; it's to allow you to work on those important tasks that you didn't have time to complete during your "mail time." Don't waste this valuable time on trivial tasks. If you have scheduled correctly, you will not have more than two or three hours of "quiet time" in any one day. Make sure there are plenty of blank spaces in your planning diary each day. After all, you need plenty of time to deal with those "interruptions" that you have defended against. The point is not to ignore them. Interruptions are part of our job. What we are attempting to do is protect blocks of time — meetings with ourselves — during which time we are inaccessible to the demands of other people. But we must still meet those demands later. In fact if they are *crises,* they may even pre-empt our quiet time. But if they do, there are those "spaces" in our planning calendar where our tasks can be rescheduled.

In order to get a quiet hour, some people arrive at the office one hour before starting time — an ideal time, since there's no obligation to answer the telephone or leave your door open. It's tempting to pick up the telephone however, so to make this work you must have the willpower to ignore ringing telephones. There's also the danger of extending your working hours. If you arrive early you should then leave early.

Work expands to fill the time available for it (Parkinson's Law) so working longer hours will not necessarily make you more effective.

The best solution is to accept the fact that your time is just as valuable as anyone else's and schedule periodic "quiet hours" during regular working days.

On several occasions executives have accused me of ignoring people while I gave preferential treatment to inanimate objects such as reports, letters, and sundry paperwork. In defence of the "quiet hour," let me relate a story that was told to me of a director of a mission who was also accused of ignoring the needs of his people while giving preferential treatment to paperwork. "You call these letters and reports inanimate objects?" he exclaimed. "We have over one hundred missionaries in the field whose only access to me, to you, and to our facilities is through these letters and reports. On the other hand, you have access to me day and night, in person or by phone. These are not inanimate objects," he admonished them. "These are *people*."

The paperwork you deal with daily is also people. They deserve the same respect as a person sitting in your office, so never feel guilty about having calls screened or visitors intercepted while you give them your attention.

HOLDING THE FORT

How to have a "quiet hour" with no office. Developing the power of concentration. How to have telephone calls intercepted.

Chapter Nine

HOLDING THE FORT

It's one thing to convince yourself that quiet hours make sense, and that you should have them coincide with those blocks of time in which you have scheduled your priority tasks. But how do you physically keep those calls and drop-ins from interrupting you? After all, most of us do work in an office, amid scores of people, telephones, and equipment. Some of us don't even have offices. Some of us may be the *only* person in the office. Who screens the calls then? And what about the boss — does a closed door keep him or her out?

Well, if you have followed the advice in Chapter 4, you at least have been able to *have* a quiet hour. Now let's see just how "quiet" we can make it. Your environment does have an effect, so if you are working in an open-office concept, make it as private as possible by adding dividers and potted plants. Get out of the line of sight of people passing your desk. If your eyes meet, it's human instinct to give a word of greeting, which in turn leads to an exchange of niceties, which in turn, frequently leads to a full-fledged conversation.

You cannot afford to get sidetracked during your quiet hour, so avoid the initial eye contact. The people who really *want* to see and talk to you will peek around the partition or divider so don't be concerned about feeling antisocial. And remember, you are free to walk out from behind that divider whenever you want — hopefully not during your quiet hour. I realize it's difficult to keep your mind on your work when you are working in an open-office environment with telephones ringing, people chatting, and typewriters clattering. But you *can* do it, if you make up your mind that you are going to concentrate on what you are doing. Your ability to concentrate is increased with positive effort and reduced by allowing yourself to be diverted. It can be represented by the following formula:

$$\text{Ability to Concentrate} = \frac{\text{Positive Effort}}{\text{Diversion}}$$

Keep the positive effort high by consciously focusing your thoughts on the job at hand. It is amazing how much of the environment you can shut out of your mind when you are highly motivated to get on with the job. Have an organized work area with all the information and tools necessary to get the job done. Hang a sign that says "Quiet Hour" or "My Door is Closed" when you are working on specific projects. And be aware that your susceptibility to diversion increases the longer you're at the job. Don't schedule too long a period without a break. Get away from your desk periodically and clear the cobwebs. Schedule the most difficult tasks when you're at your peak, perhaps first thing in the morning.

You can be productive in spite of a lack of privacy once you set your mind to it.

For those exceptionally important tasks that require complete quiet, try moving your materials into an empty office or boardroom. The telephone can be answered by someone else during this period. Let's face it, how does the organization operate when you're sick or on holidays? One hour here and there is not nearly as disruptive. And continually working under pressure amid a barrage of diversions can *make* you sick. Try the buddy system. Ask a co-worker to take your calls for one hour and you'll take their's for one hour. You'll *both* be more productive.

If you already *have* an office, all you have to do is close your door periodically. You wouldn't think of interrupting many professionals for some minor reason. When is the last time you called a surgeon during an operation, or waltzed into a teacher's classroom, or sent a message to the airline pilot during a flight? So what makes you different? A manager is a professional too, and as such deserves some interruption-free time to perform tasks. So don't hesitate to declare yourself "in session" for an hour or so at a time. Have your calls and visitors intercepted, concentrate on what you're doing, and become a more effective professional.

How do you have calls intercepted? It's important to do it correctly in order to maintain your privacy without antagonizing the callers. *Don't* have your secretary ask who's calling. If you're busy, you're busy regardless of who's calling!

If someone asks "Could I speak to John Brown please?" And the immediate response is "Could I ask who's calling?", the caller could easily get the impression that he or she is being screened to see if their name is important enough to reach the boss. If they are later told that the boss is tied up, they could be annoyed.

If you're going to have your calls intercepted at any time, quiet hour or not, do it this way: when the person asks if John Brown is there, feed back the truth immediately. "Yes, he is" or "No, he isn't" or "Yes, but he's tied up right now," followed immediately by the question, "Can I help you?" Then the caller knows that his or her name has nothing to do with the fact that the boss is tied up.

Incidentally, when *you* make a call, never force the other person's secretary to wheedle your name from you. *Announce* who's calling right at the outset. "Hello, this is Bill Smith. Could I speak to John Brown, please?" This way, you will never be insulted.

When you have a meeting with yourself, working on some priority project, treat it as you would a meeting with your boss or a major customer. Have all your calls intercepted. And don't let your secretary simply accumulate call-backs. Have her ask that magical question, "Can I help you?" Chances are she can supply the information or transfer the call to someone who can. When it's obvious that you must return the call personally, the secretary should determine the best time to reach the caller. A simple, "When is the best time to get hold of you?" will prevent a lot of telephone "ping pong." "I'll have him call you between 3:00 and 3:30" will usually result in your party being there when you call. There are standard telephone message forms. Make sure they're used. You should know what the call is about, as well as the basic information such as name, company, and phone number.

Don't make exceptions for long distance calls. Many executives will jump at the announcement, "It's long distance for you." So what? The likelihood of it being important is no greater than if the call had originated next door. Have it handled like all the rest. Your secretary should respond with the usual, "I'm sorry, he's in a meeting right now. Can I help you?" The cost of the call back, if necessary, is normally less than the value of the protected time.

If you're going to be effective as a manager you must not let yourself be victimized by the telephone. Don't let its facade of urgency fool you. Probably less than 80 percent of your calls could be classified as urgent. And, of those, over half could probably be directed to someone else.

If you absolutely refuse to have your calls intercepted, at least have your secretary advise the caller, "He's busy right now. Shall I interrupt him?" Unless it is an emergency, most callers will decline the offer. They have more respect for your time than *you* do. Alternatively, you can supply your secretary with a list of people who should be put through regardless, with everyone else being intercepted. I personally don't like this method since it gives preferential treatment to people based on their status rather than their need. Important people can make some fairly unimportant requests.

When your quiet hour is over, be sure to return those calls that could not be handled by someone else. Respect for your own time should never be confused with lack of respect for the time of others, **and make those calls yourself.** It may save a little time by having your secretary make your calls for you and then hand the party over to you once they've been contacted. But it's doubtful, considering that you had to take the time to tell your secretary who to contact in the first place. And any time saving on your part is definitely at the expense of the **other person's** because he is kept waiting on the line. Then what you're really communicating to the other party is that your time is more important than his.

Maybe your time *is* more important. And maybe

you don't mind communicating it. But at least be aware of the possible consequences. We save time in order to increase our *total* effectiveness. We don't want to lose effectiveness in another area as a result.

THE ENEMY WITHIN

How to deal with drop-ins — employees, boss or peers. Examining your own tendency to interrupt yourself and others.

Chapter Ten

THE ENEMY WITHIN

It's a relatively simple matter to have your calls intercepted. And you can generally avoid making an appointment to see clients, associates, customers, sales representatives and others at times that would conflict with your quiet hour. But what about those people who have already infiltrated the ranks? Those employees, peers, and bosses who simply barge in, closed door or not?

Well, first of all, let's take a look at your peers. A survey form, filled out by over 500 managers revealed that "interruptions by peers" was among the top ten time problems. Interestingly enough, those managers did not see *themselves* as a time problem for *their* peers. And yet we are all each others peers! We are only conscious of the times other people interrupt *us*; we are not aware of the multitude of times we interrupt *others*. So I recommend that you yourself stop interrupting your peers five, ten, or more times each day, and that you also start respecting other people's quiet hours. In the next chapter, I'll give you the tools that will help you do this. But the first step is to recognize and admit to the fact that you are a time problem to others.

People cannot change what they are unaware of, and perhaps people do not realize that they are being disrespectful. So tell them. There's nothing like good old-fashioned communication to straighten out a problem. If Frank barges in on you three or four times a day, sympathize with his need to see you, but explain that you find it difficult to work with continual interruptions. Suggest he accumulate his questions, or problems, or comments, and have them all aired during one, scheduled visit. Explain the *reason* your door is closed at certain times during the day and ask for his cooperation. A good salesperson will tell you that you get very little without asking.

It seems to be human nature to complain about something without taking positive action to change it. We excuse ourselves by claiming we don't want to hurt someone's feelings, or insult them or embarrass them. But we are doing them more harm by *not* being honest with them. We are encouraging them to be ineffective; we are gaining a low opinion of them; we may even be maligning them to others. It takes courage *and* friendship to tell someone that part of his breakfast is still adhering to his moustache, or there's shaving cream in one ear, *or* he's annoying people by his constant interruptions.

Some of the interruptions could be real crises, but there are few crises that could not wait for an hour.

We must be honest with our employees and our bosses as well. But in the case of employee interruptions, it could be *your* fault. Are you delegating properly or encouraging them to run to you with every problem? As soon as you solve a problem for them, you are encouraging them to bring more of them to you. When an employee brings a problem to you, ask "What do you suggest we do?" If they say they really haven't thought about it (why **should** they if you always supply the answer?) reply, "Well you think about it, and let me know what you suggest. I really value your opinion." Encourage employees to think for themselves. You don't have the time to do the thinking for everyone else.

It's more difficult to be honest with your boss, because he or she holds the power of hiring and firing. But no boss worth his or her salt cannot accept constructive criticism. If their constant interruptions interfere with their employees' effectiveness, it is ultimately their own effectiveness that is being diminished. Bosses are human too. So be honest with your boss and encourage your employees to be honest with you.

If your boss disregards your pleas and your suggestion of a "Delegation Record" (as described in Chapter 12) utilize the constant interruptions the best you can. Keep a folder bearing your boss's name readily at hand. Any time there is a comment, query, or approval requiring his or her attention, slip it into the folder. Every time the boss comes in, reach for that folder and have your questions resolved. You will never need to interrupt your boss — which will at least save **some** time for you. It isn't everyone who has a boss that they can always reach without ever leaving their own office or desk. If the boss gets "work" to attend to every time he or she comes near you, perhaps he or she will think twice before coming near you!

One thing that no one else **can** control, boss or otherwise, is your life. And that's what your time is. You must take responsibility for your own life. Everything you do is a trade-off. You trade two hours of life for a two hour meeting. You trade five minutes of your life for a five minute phone call. You trade two minutes of your life for a two minute interruption. So that meeting, phone call, and interruption better be valuable, because you have exchanged a part of your life for them.

Sure, you may be *paid* by a company to do certain things, but are you really selling off your life for money? Or are you trading parts of your life for a multitude of intrinsic rewards that are included in the job — such as satisfaction, a sense of achievement, mental stimulation, challenge, a feeling of worth, respect, and so on. You probably are. And if these intrinsic benefits ever cease to be part of the package deal, you should question your continued employment there. Activities that are a complete waste of time, with no benefit to either the employee or the company, are demoralizing and not worth the cost — a chunk of your life. On the other hand, if you are working in order to *survive*, since there are not other jobs available, you have no choice but to trade some of your life for money. The cost is high, but that's how "supply and demand" works. But get the best trade possible. Life's too short to waste it.

It's easy to blame other people for your time problems. But be honest with *yourself*, as well as with others. Time management is self-management. And if everyone would clean up his or her own act, most time problems would disappear.

THE TELEPHONE & VISITORS LOG

How to use a log to keep track of telephone calls and visits, insuring prompt action and eliminating the problem of forgetfulness.

Chapter Eleven

THE TELEPHONE & VISITORS LOG

Time is lost, money wasted, problems created, and tempers primed — all because of a reluctance or neglect on the part of managers to write things down. Most of them overestimate their memories and underestimate their busyness. And they discover, too late, that their intentions had been lost in the heat of the battle.

How could we remember to carry out that directive when we had to immediately reach for a ringing telephone? And no wonder we forgot to follow through on that telephone request with two people simultaneously bursting into our office! We hop from one task to another, dozens of thoughts spinning in our minds. When a new thought occurs we frequently interrupt what we're working on to pursue it before it escapes us. We're constantly juggling tasks and interrupting our staff. Occasionally we jot things down; but on scraps of paper, cigarette packages, and "to do" lists which get lost in the shuffle.

To be effective we must be organized, and this involves a system of recording that will eliminate the need to interrupt our employees or the task at hand

and still prevent us from forgetting those messages, directives, and ideas that rain upon us.

There are two major categories of follow-ups that tend to fall through the cracks; those received via the telephone or personal visits and those that we think of ourselves — those ideas that pop into our heads when we least expect them. For the first category, draw up a "Telephone and Visitors Log" form. Keep it simple, with space for the name, company, and telephone number of the caller. Divide the sheet into two vertical columns labelled "Nature of Business" and "Action Required." Every time you answer the phone or receive a visitor, quickly jot the information into this log, summarizing the key points on the left side and using the right side only when action is required as a result of the call. Even if the phone rings incessantly or a steady stream of visitors invade your office, you won't forget to follow up on anything. It's all there, in writing. When you have completed the task, cross out the notation on the right side of the log. A quick scan of the pages will tell you whether there's anything left undone.

Try it. Keep a binder containing these forms on your desk. Have it opened at the day's date ready for action. When you make or receive a call, automatically pull the binder in front of you and, instead of doodling on a scrap of paper as you talk, make notes in the "Nature of Business" area. You will be recording information that you may need in the future, even though you may not realize it at the time. When the person at the other end of the line makes a request, jot it down in the "Action Required" area. Record the name and company of the caller at the start or during a pause in the conversation. Before you hang up, be sure to get the phone number, even if you already have it in your directory. It only takes a second for the person to give it; it could take ten times that long for you to look it up.

Now you have the best back up system in the world. You can relate who called, when, about what, and the nature of the action requested — even months later. Can your memory do that? If requests or even the phone calls have ever slipped your mind this is not only a time saver, it is a *must*.

The form I use is shown in Exhibit 9. It has space to indicate whether the call was initiated by myself or the other party, the length of the call, and the time the call was made or received. This additional information allows me to determine the time of the day when most calls are received so I can schedule my quiet hours, lunch hours, breaks, etc. accordingly. It also flags the "long-winded" callers, or tells me that *I* am spending excessive time talking to certain individuals. You may find, as many people do, that 80 percent of your telephone time is spent talking to 20 percent of your callers.

This Telephone and Visitors Log has rescued me countless times. People tend to have short memories. They feel they have been waiting "weeks" for materials they had requested only a few days before. A typical experience, "Harold, I just received fifty folders in the mail. I asked for 100, and that was about two weeks ago!"

"Oh, I thought you had only asked for fifty. And it didn't seem that long ago."

"No, it was 100," he insisted, "and it was *at least* two weeks ago when I called you."

"I'm sorry, you're probably right. I have a terrible memory. Just a second, I'll check it out ..." While talking, I flipped the pages until I came to his call.

Exhibit 9
TELEPHONE & VISITORS LOG

NAME_____ DATE_____

COMPANY_____ TIME_____

NUMBER_____

NATURE OF BUSINESS

CALL ☐
VISIT ☐
INITIATED BY:
MYSELF ☐
OTHER PARTY ☐
TIME: _____

ACTION REQUIRED

LENGTH OF CALL MINUTES
2 4 6 8 10 12 14 16 18 20 22 24

NAME_____ DATE_____

COMPANY_____ TIME_____

NUMBER_____

NATURE OF BUSINESS

CALL ☐
VISIT ☐
INITIATED BY:
MYSELF ☐
OTHER PARTY ☐
TIME: _____

ACTION REQUIRED

LENGTH OF CALL MINUTES
2 4 6 8 10 12 14 16 18 20 22 24

"Oh, here it is. No, the call was made last Tuesday, Sam. And you *did* ask for 100 originally. But it's crossed out. Something about not including the committee members in this distribution ..."

"Oh, that's right. I forgot about that. And it was only last week?!"

"Yes, Tuesday, 10:15 A.M."

A pause, "What do you do, record all your calls?" he asked.

"Yes, I do. I have a terrible memory and I want to make sure I don't let anyone down."

Those may not have been the exact words, but I do let it be known that I make notes. It's for their benefit primarily. But it also encourages them from exaggerating or distorting the truth a little. And it's amazing how they tend *not* to exaggerate in the future!

It's embarrassing (and sometimes costly) to forget what you quoted a person during a previous conversation. Or that you even *had* a previous conversation. Some people, who now use a telephone log, told me they used to forget the name of the person before they even finished the conversation! Now, since the name is the first thing recorded, they are never embarrassed by not being able to recall the person's name at the end of the call.

Although the Telephone & Visitors Log prevents embarrassment and "protects your back," it is primaril intended to eliminate some of those time wasters caused by forgetfulness or lack of concentration or failure to listen. It's difficult *not* to listen when you are actually making notes on what is being said. And there's less likelihood that you'll be distracted by visitors walking into your office. There's an almost irresistable tendency to try to carry on two conversations at once — one conversation consisting mainly of hand motions to a drop-in visitor. If someone walks into your office uninvited while you're on the phone, ignore that person. The caller was there first. Just keep making notes until the call is finished.

Use this Telephone & Visitors Log for both incoming and outgoing calls. In the latter case you can jot down the items you wish to discuss in that left-hand section and check them off as you discuss them. This way, nothing will be forgotten and you won't have to make a second call. If the person is not in when you call and you leave a message to call you back at a specific time, write "to call back between 3 and 4" in that "Action Required" section. This will act as a flag in the event that the person doesn't call back as requested. Some people don't return calls promptly — or even at all — especially if it's information that *you* want. You may want to call again if you need the information before a certain date. How many times have you left a message, never received a call-back, and *forgot* to follow up? When you call again and *reach* your party, simply cross off that "to call back" notation and away you go.

The same form can be used when someone drops into your office (by invitation hopefully). Making a note of the request can only impress the visitor with your obvious intention of following it up.

This all sounds very easy. But be careful. You may find you "forget" to use the log. Or it gets put away somewhere. Or it's not opened and you can't be bothered going through the hassle of recording what will probably be a brief call. It takes persistance. Force yourself to use it for a week. The second week it will become easier. After that it will become a habit. And remember, habits are hard to break — even the good ones!

THE DELEGATION RECORD

How to record and follow up on assignments to ensure that they are completed on time. Balancing your employees workload, and eliminating continual interruptions.

Chapter Twelve

THE DELEGATION RECORD

Remember that scene in Chapter 2, where the manager continually interrupted his employees throughout the day? Well ask yourself how many times *you* interrupt *your* employees each day. Then ask yourself how many of those interruptions could not have been delayed for a half day or more without any detrimental effect on your organizational goals. The answer will probably be "none" or "very few." We tend to act impulsively, "before we forget". Unfortunately, in doing so we are impeding our employees productivity as well as our own.

To take care of those ideas that jump into your mind as you work away at a project, make up a "Delegation Record." Include vertical columns for tasks assigned, due date and date completed. Instead of interfering with your project *and* your employees, jot down the assignment or idea that came to you and get back to work. By the afternoon you may have accumulated a dozen or so items that you want to communicate to your staff. Cover them all in one sitting instead of one at a time as they occur. This eliminates those continual interruptions. Have a separate sheet

Exhibit 10

DELEGATION RECORD

MANAGER_____MONTH_____

Date Assigned	Assignment	Due Date	Date Completed	Comments

"INSTANT" TASKS   check box at right when completed

98

for each person reporting to you, and get a commitment as to when each assignment is to be completed. Record it under the "due date." Now there's no danger of forgetting to follow up on all those assignments. Simply scan the sheet daily. The form I use is shown in Exhibit 10.

I used to carry out "hallway" delegations. As I was walking down a hallway, the sight of someone would remind me of a job I wanted them to do. "Oh, John," I'd say, "I just remembered. Could you get a quote for me on a video play back unit? I need the cost for a report I'm writing."

"Sure, no problem," they'd answer. But I wouldn't hear from them. They would forget. Worse still, *I* would forget. And not until I decided to finish my report in time for the next day's meeting would I remember. This would happen with most of the verbal assignments I made. The people would not make a note of it — and neither would I. We'd *both* forget. When I did remember (usually too late), and called about it, I would get responses such as, "Sorry Harold. I've been terribly busy. But I have it on my list to do today," or "Funny you should call — I'm just working on it now." Would you believe it? Whenever I called to question a job that hadn't been completed yet, they were either working on it or about to work on it. I was psychic! Imagine *always* calling at that precise moment after having forgotten about it for over a week.

I couldn't help asking myself if they would have been "just working on it" had I called three or four days earlier. Sure enough, when I started using the "Delegation Record," that's precisely what happened. Each morning I would check my Delegation Record for any assignments due that day. Then I would phone right away. I don't believe in waiting until the day after the assignment is due and then asking if they have done it. Chances are they haven't done it or I'd have it. That's what I call playing "I gottcha." It only embarrasses the employee since they have to admit they didn't do it and come up with excuses why they didn't. And it's already too late to get it on time. Instead, the morning of the due date I say, "Jack, I realize it's early in the day, but I was just wondering if you anticipate any trouble getting that job to me today — you know, the copy department summary?"

"Oh no. No problem. In fact, I'm just working on it now." The same answer I used to get a week after it was due! They still may have forgotten it, but my call reminded them. They saved face. I got my project on time. Everybody's happy.

They may *not* have forgotten, however. For I noticed another change when I started using the Delegation Record. Whenever I asked them when they thought they could get a task done, and I wrote down their answer, *they* would make a note as well. If *I* thought it was important enough to write down, *they* thought it was important as well. And consequently there was less chance of them forgetting.

You should make one thing clear to your employees; if they are unable to complete an assignment by the agreed upon date, they must let you know *before* the due date, not after. If everyone schedules tasks on a planning diary well in advance, they should know *in advance* whether a task has to be rescheduled. Don't accept comments like, "I'm sorry, but things were really hectic last week so I couldn't get project 'A' done." Assuming you have negotiated a reasonable deadline, they should be able to say instead, "Things are really getting hectic this week; I don't think I'll be

100

able to complete project 'A' by Friday as planned."
Knowing in advance allows you to reschedule projects
if the one due Friday is a priority one. Or to advise
your boss or customer of the change in plans if it's
not.

The form I use has a column for "Comments." Use
it if you want to keep track of your employee's performance. Was the job complete, well done, creative,
submitted early or late, finished with the aid of others?
This becomes a handy reference at performance ap-
praisal time.

The "Instant Tasks" section at the bottom of the
form is for those little tasks that only take a minute or
two to complete, requests such as "check flight
times," "write to Bob Wilson," "call printers re lead
time." It's not necessary to assign a deadline for these
items. You expect them to be done that day or within
a day or two at the most. Including them among the
delegations will only clutter up the form. On a daily
basis, when you are either making assignments or follow-ups, you would ask about these items, placing a
check mark beside the items completed.

Don't lose sight of the fact that *you* may be the one
who has to take action in some of those sudden inspirations. Schedule specific times for them in your daily
planning diary. The shorter "instant tasks" can be recorded as a "things to do" list in the same planner, in
the left hand column (Refer back to Exhibit 6).

An added advantage of maintaining a Delegation
Record is that it highlights how many tasks you are as-
signing to the various people reporting to you. I was
amazed at the number of jobs I was passing along to
one person. Seeing the jobs in black and white was a
revelation. Because one particular person was reliable,
never complained, or just couldn't say "no," she was

on the receving end of most of my requests. I had to change my ways in order to balance the workload. One thing we cannot afford to do as managers is to further develop our better people while ignoring the less skilled ones.

It's not only important to write things down, but to do it in an organized manner. Develop the habit of recording your calls, visits, delegations, and other ideas that occur. Those two forms in a three-ring binder, combined with a daily planning calendar, will keep you from overlooking, misplacing or forgetting ideas, tasks and assignments that would put a strain on your effectiveness.

THE PERSONAL ORGANIZER

Keeping records in an organized manner. A telephone directory at your fingertips. How to use a planning diary effectively.

Chapter Thirteen

THE PERSONAL ORGANIZER

When I developed the Telephone & Visitors Log and Delegation Record forms, I placed them in a binder which I now refer to as my "Personal Organizer." Then I added a telephone directory when I realized how much time I was wasting looking up telephone numbers.

Most people actually keep business cards, even though they are quickly outdated and difficult to organize. I used to have a desk drawer filled with them. And I used to think I was organized if I had them divided into piles with elastic bands around them! Can you imagine trying to find a specific card? I would play "search and find" every time I wanted to retrieve one. Then, once I had used it (unsuccessfully in many cases because people are always changing jobs), I would toss it back in the drawer so I would waste more time later. And we're actually *encouraged* to keep business cards. Stores sell little file boxes and plastic window folders so we can hold onto these little time wasters.

Most telephone directories are not much better.

Exhibit 11

TELEPHONE DIRECTORY

NAME — COMPANY — ADDRESS	DESCRIPTION	TELEPHONE NUMBERS
....		Business: .... Home: ....
....		Business: .... Home: ....
....		Business: .... Home: ....
....		Business: .... Home: ....
....		Business: .... Home: ....
....		Business: .... Home: ....
....		Business: .... Home: ....
....		Business: .... Home: ....
....		Business: .... Home: ....
....		Business: .... Home: ....

There is never enough space for the frequently used letters of the alphabet; numbers become outdated; the directory becomes dog-eared or torn, and we are forever faced with the overwhelming task of copying the entire directory over again. There are better ones, but most of them fill up quickly, are difficult to update, or are not portable. I want my directory to travel with me, and a slab of metal or plastic is not the most convenient travelling companion.

I drew up the form shown in Exhibit 11 which includes a column to record the type of business the person is in (or a physical description of the person). By adding a set of alphabetical tabs to the Personal Organizer, these sheets could be included in any quantity. If I run out of space under the "A"s or "B"s I need only add more sheets. If the directory becomes outdated I only have to copy over one page at a time. The telephone directory is always with me when I'm talking on the telephone. Numbers can be transferred easily from the Telephone & Visitors Log to the Directory.

You can make up your own Personal Organizer using a three-ring binder, making up forms similar to those described, and buying dividers and alphabetical tabs from a stationery store. Or you can purchase a smaller, portable Personal Organizer from Time Management Consultants, Inc., 2175 Sheppard Avenue E., Suite 110, Willowdale, Ontario, M2J 1W8. This smaller version which has pockets for letters, postage stamps, and business cards, is shown in Exhibit 12. It is the same size as the "Taylor Time Planner®" and is available with matching cover.

If you have ever forgotten to follow up on assignments, have interrupted your staff and peers several times a day, failed to take note of a telephone number or had a telephone request "slip your mind," develop

Exhibit 12

The Personal Organizer

or buy a Personal Organizer. You will eliminate a handful of time wasters. Don't rely on your memory and don't resort to scraps of paper. Make notes in an organized manner.

The indispensable time management tool which works hand in hand with the Personal Organizer is the planning diary. Get yourself a good one and use it properly. Planning diaries come in all shapes and sizes. I developed the Taylor Time Planner because it suits *my* needs. Your needs may be different. I want a diary that is portable. I used to use a large multi-ringed diary that remained on my desk, plus a small pocket calendar that I referred to while travelling or at meetings. But invariably I would record appointments and meetings in the pocket calendar and forget to transfer the information into the desk calendar. And those oversights cost me more than simply time! Now I carry the 6-1/4" x 9-1/2" diary in my briefcase (or in my hand if I'm simply walking into another person's office) and record all my appointments and follow-ups directly into it. In my suit jacket I carry only the *cover* of a pocket calendar. it serves two purposes; it makes me look *normal*, because everyone else carries one, and it also holds index cards, blank cheques, business cards, and a set of condensed personal and company goals.

If I'm at an evening dinner party or I'm on my way to the washroom, I don't carry my 6-1/4" x 9-1/2" planning diary! Instead, I jot a note to myself on one of the index cards and shove it in the side pocket of my jacket. I have yet to miss transferring it to my planning diary because I'm forever reaching into my pocket for one thing or another. And you can't miss a 3" x 5" index card.

Since I carry my planning diary with me when I

leave the office or travel, each week I photocopy my week's plan and give it to the people who report to me. In addition, I maintain a wall calendar which records the annual activities such as business trips, seminars, vacations, etc. for the entire year.

I recommend you schedule personal activities in your planning diary as well. The Taylor Time Planner allows recording from 8:00 A.M. in half-hour graduations. You can record your children's basketball or football games, graduation days, parent-teacher meetings, golf games, and those promised quiet evenings with your spouse, family or friends. This habit has prompted reactions such as "Isn't that carrying organization a little too far — even scheduling leisure time?!" Well I don't think so, because at one time I never scheduled leisure time, and I *never* got any! There's always some business demand ready to encroach on my personal time if I give it a foothold.

Write as much information as possible into your planning diary: names, addresses, phone numbers, locations, cities, hotels, materials required at meetings, flight numbers, restaurants visited. Enter special events such as birthdays, anniversaries, weddings. Flag them with small colored self-adhesive labels. Record those necessary but low priority "things to do" in the left hand portion of the diary under the appropriate heading. When you record a "phone" reminder, include the telephone number so it's easier to follow through later. Sketch maps of how to get to meetings in an unfamiliar location. Jot down expenses, mileage. The more information you are able to record, the more useful your planning diary will be — both now and *after the fact* — when you want to recall where you've been, who you met, what you did, and what you spent.

Don't generate more paperwork than necessary, and keep the number of forms to a minimum. There'll be enough room in your planning diary for most information you will want to record. Use the "follow-up" section at the top of each day's column to flag important items. If you really want something to stand out, write it on a small yellow "Post-it" note (3M Company) and stick it right on top of the day's schedule.

You could also note when typing and other assignments are due by jotting them in this follow-up section — in red or some other color so they stand out. (Always jot the due date on any assignment given to an employee).

The current year at a glance is included near the front of the diary and next year at a glance near the end. Note all major events such as field trips, vacations, seminars, etc. here first, then record all the details in the appropriate day's column in the week at a glance section. Use the cover flaps to hold colored labels. Split a "Post-it" pad into about four or five parts and stick them to the inside of the back or front cover, ready for use.

These tools will help keep you organized. But only if you are willing to get into the habit of using them. Which means you will have to develop a little self-discipline.

BUILDING SELF-DISCIPLINE

How to form good time management habits, concentrate on tasks at hand, and build self-discipline into your workday.

Chapter Fourteen

BUILDING SELF-DISCIPLINE

All interruptions aren't caused by other people. We probably interrupt **ourselves** more than we're interrupted by others. This may sound unreasonable, but it isn't when you add up all those minutes wasted through daydreaming, sudden "inspirations" that detract us from the job at hand, the seeming need for a coffee or a stretch, fatigue and boredom which causes us to stall, and our susceptibility to disturbances around us, whether it be noise or motion.

Many times we actually **welcome** interruptions whether we admit it or not. And it all boils down to lack of concentration on our part.

But how do you concentrate when you've been writing a report for two hours or weeding through priority paperwork or some overwhelming task that seems to have no end?

Well, here are a few suggestions:

(1)   *Dig right in.* The hardest part of any task is getting started. We procrastinate. Fidget. Rearrange our working materials. Grab a coffee. The law of physics that states that a body at

rest tends to stay at rest and a body in motion tends to stay in motion is true for humans as well. Once you get started, you'll gain some headway. So muster all your willpower and decide to dig right in with a minimum of delay. If it's writing you're doing, start to write regardless of whether the first sentences make sense. You will have at least primed the pump, and you can make revisions later. You can develop a "dig right in" habit. Try it.

(2) *Get your second wind.* Working is like running — push yourself that extra mile and you'll get a second wind. Don't yield to the first temptation to take a break. Be determined to finish one more page of that report, or two more letters before taking a break. Set a goal of one half hour, or two hours, and stick to it. Concentration improves when it's directed towards a goal. If there's a reward at the end, such as a coffee break or a ten minute stretch so much the better.

(3) *Tackle the job in reasonable chunks.* Don't expect to retain concentration on an all-day project. The longest concentration span for most of us is less than two hours. If you have a three- or four-hour task, break it up into one- or two-hour sessions with a completely different activity in between.

(4) *Keep an "idea sheet" handy.* Regardless of your ability to concentrate, you won't prevent those ideas from popping into your head (which usually have no connection whatever to the task at hand). Don't try to ignore them; they could be valuable. But don't let them sidetrack you either. Keep a pad of paper handy and jot down

those thoughts for later action. Then, back to the task. Most of us let these ideas sidetrack us to the point where we walk out of the room or grab for the telephone in order to follow them up before we forget them.

(5)   *Guard against boredom, fatigue.* We tend to interrupt ourselves simply because we're uncomfortable. Have a stand-up desk handy so you can quickly change positions. Or move to a table. Failing that, at least take a thirty-second stretch every half hour or so.

It takes willpower and practice to be able to concentrate on a task while noise and activity surround us. But with effort it will become a habit — like reading the paper with the T.V. set blaring. Your mind can only be one place at a time, so make sure it's concentrating on the job at hand.

Managing your time involves a lot of self discipline. And self-discipline is *making yourself do something that doesn't come naturally.* For example, if you have been getting up at 7:30 A.M. every day for the last fifteen years, it's not natural to get up at 6:30 A.M. You have to set the alarm and then *make yourself get up.* It's hard work. But eventually you will form a new habit. And a habit is something you do naturally.

The same thing applies to going on a diet, engaging in a regular fitness program, giving up three cups of coffee and a morning newspaper, leaving the T.V. set turned off after dinner, and so on.

So much is dependent upon self-discipline, that if you are really serious about gaining control of your time, you're going to have to face one fact: initially, *it's hard work.* And no number of time saving gimmicks, or systems will change that fact.

Most managers blame other people for their time

problems. Well, *you* are everyone else's *"other people,"* so take a good look at your own habits. Do you interrupt your peers or employees when *you* feel like socializing? Do you linger at the coffee pot in the mornings, striking up conversations with everyone? Do you pick up the intercom or phone to the same person several times during the day instead of accumulating the question or ideas? Do you drag out telephone calls, visits, or meetings? Do you write letters when a phone call will do? Do you leave messages to call you back and then disappear from the office? Do you circulate junk mail with vague notations such as "Please note"? Do you give your secretary letters marked "A.S.A.P." instead of specifying a date? Do you leave the office without telling people when you'll be back? Are you a perfectionist? A procrastinator?

Habits are activities that we carry out without the necessity of forethought or conscious effort. Driving a car, signing cheques, lighting up a cigarette, are all examples of habits. If you want to form a habit, repeat something over and over again. Eventually it becomes second nature. Almost automatic.

Try forming some time management habits. Like scheduling all important activities directly into your planning calendar. Starting the day by working on the most important project. Dispensing with your mail by handling each item only once. Using checklists before meetings, trips. Each month select one good time management practice and repeat it each day until it becomes a habit. Good habits and bad habits both have one thing in common. They're hard to break.

OVERCOMING PROCRASTINATION

How to overcome the tendency to put off unpleasant or overwhelming tasks. Getting an early start and maintaining momentum.

Chapter Fifteen

OVERCOMING PROCRASTINATION

One habit that impedes success deserves special attention. *Procrastination.* It devours our time and keeps us from accomplishing those important personal and organizational goals. Lick this one, and you're well on your way to success.

Someone once commented. "Procrastination is the only thing I have time for!" And it's so true. We always find plenty of excuses to put something off. Either we don't have time to do it right now, or we're waiting for more information or we feel tired, ad infinitum. We'll shuffle papers, engage in small talk, get coffee, straighten our desks, make "one last call" or promise ourselves we'll start first thing in the morning. As a result, important tasks get delayed, goals aren't reached, effectiveness drops. We feel guilty about not getting it done. We get uptight. We can't concentrate on the job we are doing. We get discouraged. Depressed. Procrastination is not only the thief of time, it's the thief of our success as well. It must be understood — and eliminated.

There are some legitimate reasons for procrastinating. Perhaps we *don't* have enough information to make a decision. Or perhaps our hands are tied until someone else carries out *their* responsibilities. But in most cases we procrastinate because it's either an overwhelming task that would take hours or days to complete, or it's a distasteful task that we wish we could avoid altogether.

Let's take a look at the overwhelming task first. Perhaps it's something that would take at least three hours to complete. And you just don't *have* three hours today. So you deceive yourself into thinking you'll have three hours "later," and do nothing. But three hours of free time never comes. Your days fill up with "busyness" — interruptions, telephone calls, visitors, meetings — and you keep delaying that important project that means so much to your success.

The only way to avoid procrastination, is to *start* the task, regardless of whether you've got five minutes or five hours of free time. Estimate how long the job will take and schedule blocks of time in your planning calendar. Commit yourself to working on the task during those scheduled blocks of time. Try to schedule as much time as possible for each "sitting." You can get a lot more productive work done in sixty minutes than you can in six sittings of ten minutes each. These large, important tasks are seldom urgent when they first appear — they only *become* urgent after we've put off doing them for a while. So schedule these blocks of time as soon as the job appears. That way you'll be able to plan farther into the future and reserve large intervals of time (one or two hours) before your planning calendar becomes filled with other activities.

If, for some reason, you cannot free yourself for an hour, or even a half hour at a time, use what Alan Lakein (author of *How To Get Control of Your*

Time and Your Life) refers to as the "swiss cheese" method. Work on the task for five minutes today, five minutes tomorrow, making small "holes" in your overwhelming task until it looks like a swiss cheese and finally disappears altogether. When you come right down to it, there's no such thing as an overwhelming task — only a series of small tasks which **collectively** add up to what appears to be an overwhelming task. For example, I don't write a book, I write a series of chapters. And I don't write a chapter at one sitting. I write one section. Each section is a series of paragraphs, and so on. It doesn't take six months to write a book. It takes one hour — again and again. Similarly you don't have to spend all day cleaning out the garage. You simply spend a half hour each day or each weekend cleaning off a few shelves or a tool cabinet — and eventually the whole garage is cleaned out. You can apply this same technique to the writing of reports, reading books, redecorating a house, saving money for a trip to Europe, improving personal skills, meeting all the members of your church. Almost any large task or activity can be broken down into smaller increments. If you don't approach large tasks this way, the very thought of doing them will overwhelm you. And you'll never get started.

If you're skeptical of this approach, think for a moment about the tasks you **don't** want to be completed. The cord of wood for your fireplace for instance. Seems like a lot of wood. But one stick at a time, and before you know it, you're out buying more. If you have children around the house, you'll realize that no task is unsurmountable. Huge tubs of ice cream and pails of peanut butter seem to disappear overnight — yet are tackled only one scoop at a time.

And look at life itself. Only a second passes at a

time and yet too soon we are forty, fifty and sixty years old, and getting older all the time. Amazing what a series of seconds can do.

Make this "swiss cheese" method a part of your life. A college degree is obtained one credit at a time. A thousand clients are obtained one client at a time. And your life-time goals are reached one step at a time. Don't let any task overwhelm you. And don't even *think* about procrastinating. Think only about *doing.*

In addition to those big jobs we don't have time for are those *little* jobs that are unpleasant. The phone call we have to make to cancel an order. The interview with the boss to ask for a raise. The dismissal of an employee. The visit to the dentist. The visit to an influential businessman to get him to endorse your product. That "cold call." That confrontation with the banker. All these things that you *have* to do, but don't *like* to do.

By putting something off we somehow hope that something will happen in the future that will eliminate the necessity of doing it. Sometimes our wish comes true — but too infrequently to justify the practice. What all too often happens is that we end up having to do it after all — under extreme pressure, at an inconvenient time, and at a high cost.

The tendency is to do the things you like to do and put off those unpleasant jobs. And the longer you put them off, the more you worry about them. They make you all uptight. You dread the day when you can put them off no longer and have to act. You're in a state of anxiety. As a result you are less effective in what you *are* doing. And the longer you wait, usually the worse it gets. And if you leave it until the last possible minute you'll have to work under increased pressure.

Whenever you put off today's tasks you add to tomorrow's burdens.

But when you *do* finally act, what a relief! It's as though an oppressive weight has been lifted from your shoulders. You feel so great you wonder why you didn't get it out of the way sooner.

Why suffer by dragging out the inevitable? You know you'll have to do it eventually, so why not do it right away and prevent a lot of anxiety and stress? Take action the minute the task makes itself known. Don't tell yourself to delay it because its unpleasant. Tell yourself to *do it now* because it's unpleasant. Get it over with. Learn by the example of the child who eats that terrible spinach first, and ends his meal with all those pleasant tasting foods. Once the spinach is down, he can enjoy the rest of the meal and take off for his playtime activities.

Don't be like the child who pushes the terrible green stuff aside, picks at his food, delaying the inevitable. The child doesn't enjoy his meal, has nothing with which to kill the taste when his mother forces him to sit and eat the vegetable, and misses half his play period.

Replace the procrastination habit with the "do it now" habit. It takes self-discipline, but you can do it. And when you do, you won't be one of those people who spends most of his time *preparing* and never getting around to really living.

There is always the odd task that is so overwhelming or distasteful that you keep putting it off *in spite* of your continued efforts to fight procrastination. You may even have scheduled it for a specific time or a specific day, but something more important "mysteriously" arises at the last minute to pre-empt it. You need to be in top form to muster enough willpower to literally *attack* the task. More than early morning "prime time" will give you. More than a "rah rah" motivational talk will give you.

But something *will* give you the power to attack that task and wipe it out, and that is the *power you get from having accomplished something significant.* Ever notice how you feel when you've succeeded in convincing the boss on a certain course of action, or sold a big order to a hard-nosed buyer, or received a promotion when several others were competing for the same position? Whenever you *succeed* at something, confidence and power well up inside you. You feel you can tackle anything. Use that power. Thats the time to tackle that tough job you haven't had the heart to tackle. Attack it, and wipe it out.

The effectiveness of your day can be predicted within the first hour. If you get off to a bad start — if you're disorganized, prone to procrastination, vulnerable to interruptions — then your day will probably follow suit. But if you are organized, if you have a daily goal, a plan and productive work habits, you will accomplish much.

Since the early hours of the morning are critical to the success of the day, the time to prepare your plan for those early hours is the afternoon or the evening before. Each night list your objectives for the following day. Schedule the activities on your daily diary. Clear your desk or work area of anything except the things needed to work on those first priority jobs. Resist the temptation to just walk away from the mess at quitting time. Chances are, if you're disorganized when you leave at night, you'll be disorganized when you return the next morning.

Psychologists have concluded that managers who leave the office with a clear idea of what they want to accomplish the next day, actually enjoy their personal lives more that evening. In contrast those who leave their desks and minds in a muddle, enjoy themselves less.

Try getting up earlier in the morning. You may be sleeping eight or more hours each night out of habit. If you need it, fine. But experiment first. If you sleep a half hour less each night you'll gain an extra week each year. But more important, you'll get an early start on the day. You'll have time to review your day's plans. And ask yourself whether what you had planned for that day will really lead you closer to your goals. You'll also have time to change those plans if circumstances have changed in the meantime.

Don't start the day with activity. Though many of us are action-oriented, dying to get into the thick of things — doing instead of thinking, the greatest productivity gains are made not by doing more work, but by eliminating unnecessary work. We must look before we leap. Getting to work early ahead of the other people allows us the opportunity to select the real priorities of the day — and to get them done before other people even start theirs.

There's a proverb that tells us "as the first hour of the day goes, so goes our day." Believe it. Don't allow yourself to procrastinate at this crucial period in the day. The temptation is great because the real priority tasks are often the most difficult, time-consuming or distasteful. Dig right into that arduous task and get it over with. Most of us have a tendency to delay that first early morning task. We use coffee and greeting rituals as our excuse. Or the morning newspaper. Or mail.

Realize that the longer you delay something, the more pressure you'll be working under — and the more things there are that can go wrong.

Build up some early morning momentum and you'll be able to coast through the day with less difficulty. Overcome your daily inertia with a burst of early morning enthusiasm. Once you get rolling, you can plow through those daily tasks and achieve your daily objectives.

But above all, make sure you *have* daily objectives. Don't look at today as an extension of yesterday. Look upon it as an independent unit of time. Set daily goals that tie into your weekly, monthly, and annual goals. Judge your performance on a daily basis. Before you quit each night determine whether you accomplished what you set out to do that morning.

Get up early. Don't get sidetracked. Dig right into that priority task. Review accomplishments. If you can do this on a continual basis, you will have no trouble getting started in the mornings, and your tendency to procrastinate will be a thing of the past.

MANAGING YOUR EMOTIONS

The devastating and time wasting effects of emotions such as anger and worry and how to control them.

Chapter Sixteen

MANAGING YOUR EMOTIONS

It's good to blow off steam once in a while, they tell us. That way, it's not bottled up inside us, building up pressure. Explode once in a while and it dissipates harmlessly.

Harmless to whom? A shotgun going off or a bomb exploding rarely dissipates harmlessly. Someone is usually injured in the process. People are murdered, car accidents occur, suicides take place, lives are ruined — all because of emotions such as anger and hatred being vented. Reports indicate that one out of every three car accidents are caused by angry drivers. Reacting to a situation with anger is like pouring gasoline on a fire. And the resulting time loss is phenomenal.

But what can we do? Absorb the insults, incompetence, pressures, innuendos, frustrations, that we encounter at work and at home with a "grin and bear it" attitude? Are we supposed to be men and women made of steel, letting life's bombs bounce off us like pellets off armour plate? Should we keep all that anger and frustration and worry inside us until it finally bursts free in the form of ulcers, heart attack or illness? After all, specialists in the field or psychosomatic medicine believe that from 50 percent to 80 percent of all physical ills originate in the emotions. How can we possibly cope?

What we must do, is manage our emotions. And managing our emotions does not involve either letting them fester and swell inside us or releasing them with a vengeance. It involves recognizing that we are angry or upset or worried and dealing with our feelings sensibly. Having angry feelings is okay. It's our *response* to those feelings that makes the difference. Anger is usually accompanied by thoughts of how to get even. It can motivate a person to hate, tease, humiliate, criticize or offend another person. Don't let your "okay" feeling elicit a "not okay" response.

Instead, after you have recognized that you feel angry or upset, talk it out. Initially this talk should be with *yourself*. Admit to yourself that you are angry, not because of what someone did or said, but because of how you *reacted* to what they did or said. Accept the fact that no *person* can make you angry, or happy or sad. People cannot manufacture an emotion inside another person. You are the only one who has the power to form an emotion within yourself. And similarly, *you* are the only one who can dissipate it. Ask yourself what affect the person's remark or act will have on your life? How will your financial, personal, and business status be changed? How important will the incident be one year from now?

This will put things in perspective, and generally reduce the remark or act that angered you to one of insignificance.

Next, confront the individual. Tell him or her that you feel angry, or hurt or annoyed over their remark or act. Explain why. You may be surprised at the response. You may find that you misinterpreted their remark or misunderstood the reason for their action. Or perhaps they already regret it because they had acted without thinking or were responding emotionally themselves and welcomed this opportunity to apologize.

Don't strike back in blind fury, and don't let the emotion fester inside you. Talk it over with yourself first, and the offender second. And do this quickly. The Bible tells us "Do not let the sun go down while you are still angry." Good advice for anyone.

Worry is another time-wasting emotion. "Don't worry" they tell you. Easier said than done. Your son is already an hour late getting home, you were supposed to meet the Smith's fifteen minutes ago, and your telephone is out of order. As if tonight's events aren't enough you anticipate the announcement of a massive lay off at the plant on Monday, your mortgage is coming due next month, and you have already decided you have to cancel the non-cancellable trip to Florida and lose your deposit.

Worry for some people is a way of life. There seems to be so many things to worry about nowadays. And they get totally caught up in an emotion that not only wastes time, but damages their health. It could result in migraines, ulcers, burnout, emotional breakdown or worse.

Think back for a moment over the events of this past week. Then ask yourself a question: "How much time did I spend worrying?" Once you have the estimate, ask yourself another question: "What did my worrying accomplish?"

Nothing positive is ever accomplished through worry. *Concern* is a different matter. There's nothing wrong with being concerned when your son is an hour late getting home, or your car won't start, or you don't have enough money to pay the mortgage. Concern prompts you to take action to rectify the situation. Concern shows that you're human. Concern is justified. But a person who blows a real or imagined problem way out of proportion and allows it to control their thoughts to the point that they can never get it out of their mind, is not only concerned, he's *worried*.

If worry doesn't accomplish anything, how can we stop ourselves from worrying? The first thing we have to do is recognize that we tend to think the worst. Studies indicate that 40 percent of our worries are about things that never happen. Another 30 percent of our worries concern things that are in the past and we would be unable to do anything to change them anyway. Twelve percent of our worries are needless concerns about health, probably due to our overactive, and pessimistic, imaginations.

Ten percent of our worries are petty, miscellaneous worries. *Only 8 percent of our worries are about real, legitimate concerns.*

So put your problem into perpective. Recognize the fact that some of your fears could be unfounded. Which brings us to the next suggestion — think positively. Nothing is as defeating as a negative attitude. Sure, your son could be late because of a car accident. But he could have run out of gas, or stopped for a pizza, or decided to drop in on a friend on the way home. Your client may not have returned a telephone call because he's not interested in doing business with you anymore. But he also could have been called out of the office unexpectedly or be tied up in a meeting or have forgotten about the message. Whenever you're confronted with something of concern, immediately think of three or four positive possibilities. You might as well approach life with a positive attitude, since 92 percent of the worries are unnecessary anyway.

What if there's nothing positive about the situation? What if it's a definite disaster? In that case, worry is still futile. You must distinguish between what you can and cannot control. If there's something you can do to change the situation or prevent something from happening, do it. Action dissipates worry. Alternatively, worry tends to debilitate us. It inhibits productive activity and drains our resource of energy.

So take action immediately. If it's impossible to take action, if it's completely beyond your control, worry is still futile. Take solace in the fact that it's not the end of the world. Deal with today's problems today, but don't make it harder on yourself by taking on tomorrow's problems as well.

Whatever you do, don't let worry fester inside you. Talk it out. Discuss it with a close friend. It's surprising how much lighter a burden becomes when you vocalize it. If you have faith in God, take your problems to Him in prayer. "Cast all your anxiety on Him, because He cares for you."

Managing yourself — your habits and your emotions — is the most difficult part of personal organization. It's easy to say "set up a follow-up file" and "don't react angrily when someone dumps a pile of urgent requests on your desk." But getting in the habit of *using* the follow-up file, and convincing yourself *not* to react negatively, is another matter.

But you can do it. It takes effort; but since when did anything worthwhile become easy? The reward is worth the effort. So stick with it.

Once you have organized your environment, your working materials and yourself — and have reduced the time being spent on the time obligations — you are ready to manage your *life*. This is accomplished by thinking about your future, setting goals, and establishing an action plan to achieve them.

Goal setting is the most important priority activity of them all. Without goals it is impossible to accurately identify any other priorities, since by our definition, priorities are those activities which contribute directly to the attainment of your goals.

In the remaining chapters I will explain how to set goals. Once you set goals you will be able to identify your other priorities, and devote the time to them that you have saved through personal organization.

MANAGING YOUR LIFE

How to plan a career and decide how you want to spend the balance of the time in your life.

Chapter Seventeen

MANAGING YOUR LIFE

Time is life. And life is too valuable to waste on meaningless activities which bring little satisfaction. You'll be spending the rest of your life in the future. So don't jump into any career without first asking yourself whether it's the kind of work you want to spend your time on. Grab a pencil and paper and scribble the answers to some questions. Where do you want to be ten years from now? What do you enjoy doing most? What are your strengths? What do you think you're really good at doing? What activities in the past have been the most rewarding in terms of personal satisfaction and achievement?

Most people spend more time planning parties than they do their lives. Your life is the only real resource you've got. Everything else evolves from it. Don't take it for granted and don't throw yourself at the mercy of chance. You *can* influence your future. So don't drift through life with no particular direction or destination. Stay put for a few hours — or better still, a weekend — and take inventory of yourself. Conduct a self-appraisal. Determine your personal values. Your likes and dislikes.

Establish a set of personal and career goals. Find out where you're at and where you want to be.

Don't kid yourself into thinking you're in full control of your life until you've taken the time for this self-appraisal. It could be you're being swept along with the current, too busy making a living to really make a life. I shudder to think of people who are in jobs they don't really enjoy. Trapped by salaries, pensions, or the fear of change. Don't expend life's energy responding to the initiative of others. Develop your own. Set goals. And plan to achieve them.

The goals you set may lead you to a different organization. Or into your own business. Or you may be able to achieve success where you are. The important thing is that you have thought it out. Consciously decided where you're heading, and how you're going to get there. You have taken charge of your own life.

To remain dormant in one job, or to bounce haphazardly from one job to another with no idea of where you may end up next, is to perform a disservice to yourself and to your company.

By acquiring the habit of managing your life by objectives — by planning each step in your career — you become goal oriented, time conscious, and adept to setting priorities. You are forced to plan well into the future, acquire new skills, gain new experiences, make new business contacts and become a more valuable member of the organization.

If you occupy one of these rare positions that presents continual challenges and excitement, a position that helps develop more of your unique talents, a job that grows with you, your career planning is simplified. But normally a job is something you should plan to grow into and then out of. One of the risks you must minimize is becoming bored with life. A series of new and different jobs will allow you to continue to realize more of your potential.

When you find a job stimulating and enriching, you perform more effectively. If it becomes routine and unchallenging, your effectiveness drops.

When planning your career, you must decide how much time and energy you are willing to spend. Your career should satisfy your financial needs, your individual needs, and your family's needs. The sacrifices that workaholics make, in terms of their personal lives, do not seem worthwhile to most of us.

You may not want to aim for the very top. You might meet a lot of workaholics there.

But that's where your personal goals come in. Personal goals determine the direction you take in life and involve not only your job but your family relationships, spiritual and social needs, self development needs and your personal values. Career path planning is but one part of it, but an essential part. No matter how much companies talk about it, career path planning is the individual's problem. The individual is the only one who really knows his desires, strengths, weaknesses, and motivations.

THE GOAL-SETTING PROCESS

How to establish life goals and plan your future so the passage of time will result in predetermined accomplishments.

Chapter Eighteen

THE GOAL-SETTING PROCESS

It's not enough to *think* about your future. You must reduce your goals to writing. But don't be too precise initially. Dream a little. Project yourself ten years into the future and using Exhibit 13, as a guide, visualize where you'll be, assuming you continue as you are, without making any significant changes in your life. In ten years, how old will you be? What job will you have? What will your income be? What's your family situation? What are your most important possessions? And so on. Are you happy with what you see? If not, project yourself into the future again, this time assuming you can achieve anything you want to achieve, and be anything you want to be. You don't have to be realistic at this stage. It's simply a way of forcing yourself to put things down on paper. So when you record your *accomplishments,* you could have written ten books, travelled around the world, been elected to a government post, started up your own company, and purchased a beautiful vacation home on some tropical island. This exercise forces you to express, *in writing,* all your dreams of a lifetime.

Exhibit 13

TAKE A LOOK AT THE FUTURE

It is 10 years from now. You have achieved your dreams of a decade ago. Your personal circumstances have changed. Take inventory of yourself.

Date _____   Age _____

Occupation _____

Specific Responsibilities _____

_____

_____

Annual Income: _____

Most important personal possessions _____

_____

_____

Family situation (age, occupation, education etc. of your wife and children)

_____

_____

_____

_____

Hobbies and leisure activities

_____

_____

_____

_____

Accomplishments during the past 10 years that gave the greatest sense of achievement

_____

_____

_____

_____

Next, zero in on some of those "make believe" accomplishments. How important *is* that vacation home or that trip around the world? And how realistic is it as a goal? Would attainment in fifteen years be possible? Or in twenty? If so, make a list of those things you feel could be accomplished in longer periods of time. There's no reason you shouldn't plan twenty or more years in advance.

Cross off any pie in the sky dreams. But before you do, question whether they are really pie in the sky. After all, you've got ten or more years in which to achieve them. And if you start now and work towards them, perhaps they *can* be achieved.

There are two possible sets of results. Those that would take place if you continue living as you are, maintaining the status quo, and making no effort to achieve anything in particular. Or those results that would take place if you set a specific objective and worked towards that objective, step by step, over the next ten year period. I am convinced that you can accomplish more tasks, attain greater success, and lead a more satisfying, more prosperous life if you have specific goals to aim for.

Once you have the list of things you would like to accomplish within the next ten or more years, and you are satisfied that they are attainable, you must word them so that they are measurable. "To save a lot of money" is not measurable. To save $50,000 by December 31, 1995, *is* measurable.

And it can be broken down into annual and monthly goals, which collectively add up to the long-range goal of $50,000.

If you have an intangible goal, such as happiness, personal growth, popularity, etc., you must convert it to a tangible, measurable goal. Using Exhibit 14 as a

Exhibit 14

**WORKSHEET FOR CONVERTING AN INTANGIBLE GOAL
TO TANGIBLE ONES**

1. Intangible goal:

_____

_____

2. Specific activities which would help achieve this goal:

_____

_____

_____

_____

_____

_____

_____

_____

_____

3. Convert each activity to a tangible measurable goal:

_____

_____

_____

_____

_____

_____

_____

_____

_____

_____

_____

_____

_____

_____

Exhibit 15

**EXAMPLE OF CONVERTING AN INTANGIBLE GOAL
TO TANGIBLE ONES.**

1. Intangible goal:
   Personal growtn

2. Specific activities which would help achieve this goal:

   (a) Management training, upgrading of skills

   (b) Community leadership

   (c) Public speaking engagements

   (d) Knowledge of public affairs, diverse subjects

   (e) Increased business contacts, friendships

3. Convert activities to tangible measurable goals:

   (a) Complete a Certificate course in Management and Administration by April, 1987

   (b) Attend 6 full-day seminars on specific management skills by May 31, 1984

   (c) Assume position as officer of Jaycees by December 31, 1984

   (d) Assume position on board of directors of Canadian Institute of Management by May 31, 1985

   (e) Complete Dale Carnegie course on public speaking by December 31,1986

   (f) Read, and summarize, a minimum of 24 books by December 31, 1984

   (g) Join the Personnel Association of Toronto and the Ontario Society for Training & Development and attend a minimum of 8 dinner meetings by May 31, 1986 guide, list the specific activities that would help achieve the intangible goal, and convert those activities to tangible, measurable goals. Exhibit 15 illustrates how this might be done for the intangible goal of "personal growth."

It won't take ten years, or even five years to achieve some of your goals. So break them down into long-range goals (over five years), intermediate-range goals (one to five years) and short-range goals (one month to a year). Draw up forms similar to Exhibit 16, and list your intermediate-range and short-range goals.

Be sure to consider family, spiritual, and self-improvement goals as well as business or job goals. Place deadlines on all your goals, otherwise it's too easy to procrastinate. Achieving short range goals should bring you closer to your intermediate goals which in turn make a contribution to your long range goals. This "one bite at a time" method is the surest way of achieving long range goals. For example, it's so much easier to read three books a month than thirty-six books a year.

Ask yourself the question, "If I knew I was going to die in six months what would I do? How would I spend those last six months?" (See bottom of Exhibit 16.) Your answer will probably highlight some real priorities in your life, activities that may not even appear on your list of goals. If you would spend more time with your family, or take a trip to Europe, those activities must be important to you. So make sure they appear on your written goals list. You have a better chance of achieving them when you have *more* than six months to achieve them.

When reducing your goals to writing, be sure that they are challenging, but realistic. If they're unobtainable, they lose their motivational value. They

Exhibit 16

WHAT WOULD YOU LIKE TO ACCOMPLISH
WITHIN THE NEXT THREE YEARS?

1.

2.

3.

4.

5.

6.

7.

8.

IF YOU KNEW YOU WERE GOING TO DIE IN SIX MONTHS......

What things would you do? How would you live? (Take everything into consideration, including your family and job)

1.

2.

3.

4.

5.

6.

should also be specific and definite, clearly measurable in terms of dollars, units, etc. complete with the time set for their accomplishment. Rank them in order of priority and be sure they don't conflict with one another, or with your family's goals.

In fact, involve your family in the goal-setting process. They all have a stake in your future. And they play a big part in supporting your efforts.

Be aware of the consequences of pursuing the different goals, and accept the fact that everything doesn't come easy.

PLANNING TO ACHIEVE

How planning will take you from where you are to where you want to be. Keeping your goals flexible.

Chapter Nineteen

PLANNING TO ACHIEVE

Don't expect to achieve your goals without adequate planning. Planning moves things from where they are now to where we want them to be in the future. It translates intention into action. Planning forces us to fill our calendars with the activities which reflect our goals in life. It protects us from all those trivial tasks that tend to obscure the important ones. And it prevents crises by forseeing problem areas in advance and providing a course of action that will avoid them.

Planning ensures results. Many sales persons have multiplied profits by setting aside Friday afternoon to plan their activities for the coming week. Others set aside the first hour of each day for this purpose. Frank Bettger, in *How I Raised Myself From Failure to Success in Selling* claims he didn't succeed until he started planning his days.

Few of us deny that one hour in planning saves three in execution. Yet we don't have time to plan. And we don't have time to plan because we're caught up in the hectic, time-wasting activities, many of which result from *not* planning. We're trapped in a vicious circle.

If you don't have time to plan, or set goals, use the techniques described in this book to get organized. Grit your teeth and let the world pass you by for a few hours. You may miss a few important calls, lose a few sales, antagonize a few people. But in the end you will save more time by being organized than you stole in the first place. And your effectiveness will multiply once you schedule at least a half hour for planning each day, two hours for planning each week, and four hours for planning each month. Start by looking at your statement of where you want to be, and work backwards from that goal. Don't start the morning by asking yourself "what do I have to do today?" That will only get you involved in activities. Instead, ask yourself "what is it that I am attempting to *accomplish* today?" Most things should relate to your long-range goals.

Don't neglect the short-term *performance*. You can *plan* long-range, but can't *perform* long-range. And doing is as important as planning. So translate your long-range and short-range plans into immediate activities. Schedule those priority activities into your calendar. Leave plenty of room for those last minute emergencies. At the end of each day, determine whether you accomplished what you had set out to do in the morning.

Carry an abbreviated version of your goals with you on index cards as a constant reminder of the direction you're heading. Eventually your goals will work their way into your subconscious mind, and you will automatically make the daily decisions best suited to their achievement.

As part of your planning process, have an annual review of your goals and make changes where necessary. Your goals are not carved in stone. They can be changed as your situation changes. Many people refuse to plan their future because they are afraid of being locked into a rigid, predetermined course of action. Well, goals are not supposed to be rigid and unyielding. They simply add purpose and direction to life. Without them, we drift.

One of the problems with the philosophy, "eat drink and be merry for tomorrow we may die" is that we may not! Life expectancy has come a long way — from about forty in 1850 to about seventy at the present time.

And goals may very well help to *extend* our lifespan. The quickest way to end a lifetime is to retire and do nothing. With no goals — nothing to live for — retired people waste away quickly. Unfortunately, too few people plan for their retirement until it's almost upon them, and by that time it's too late. Planning at any stage is better than no planning at all, but ideally the time to start preparing for retirement is before you reach forty. Financial planning should start long before the salary cheque stops. Watch you don't run out of money before you run out of life.

And retirement is a beginning of a new stage in your life, not an ending. It's a time to do things that got shoved aside while building a career and raising a family. If retirement is looming ahead of you right now, don't be afraid of it. Look at it as an opportunity. It could be the most productive period of your life. Your energy will increase as you work towards specific goals.

KEEP YOUR LIFE IN BALANCE

How to avoid burn-out and maintain a balance between your career and your personal life.

Chapter Twenty

KEEP YOUR LIFE IN BALANCE

Keep your job — and your life — in perspective. With so much emphasis on success and achievement it sometimes becomes difficult to relax and enjoy life. Don't set your sights too high. Do the best you can, but don't kill yourself. Job burn-out is a result of too much stress, and most jobs are stressful enough without adding your own unrealistic goals and expectations.

Set realistic goals. And realize that you can't do everything. Work on priorities — the 20 percent of the activities which will bring you 80 percent of the results.

And always have some way of working off mental and emotional stress. Engage in a regular exercise program. Have interests other than your job. Make it a habit to talk over your problems with a close friend.

Above all, remember that what you *are* is more important that what you *do*.

It's possible that you work harder and faster under the pressure of unrealistic deadlines, but it's doubtful that you work *better*. Excellence does not come from tired, harried people. Mediocrity does. You would hate to have your plane piloted by someone who had been flying steadily for twelve hours. And you probably wouldn't feel too comfortable in a taxi if the driver had been driving all night. It's a fact that tired workers cause accidents. For the same reason, most skiing mishaps take place during that "one last run."

Don't talk yourself into believing that working steadily with your nose to the grindstone will lead to success. It will only lead to a flat nose. Work smarter, not harder. Concentrate on the goals you set for yourself. Every day do something to bring yourself closer to them. But recognize that you will have to ignore some of those unimportant activities that produce minimal results. You can't do everything and still keep your life in balance.

Many managers, particularly entrepreneurs, keep putting off their vacations; in some cases skipping them altogether. This is a mistake. Vacations should be blocked off in your calendar ahead of anything else. Relaxation is necessary in order to keep your mind alert, your body healthy, and your family together.

Some managers take better care of their office equipment and plant machinery than they do their own bodies. The human body is a lot more valuable than a hunk of machinery, and with a little care it may have a longer life. But one thing it doesn't have is a warranty or money-back guarantee. There are no returns or allowances. So spend all the time and money necessary for preventive maintenance.

To prevent yourself from filling your planning calendar with only work-related activities, schedule blocks of leisure time. Those outings with the children, that movie with your spouse, that tennis game or shopping trip. Schedule them in ink, not pencil; make them definite, not tentative. Most people schedule them with the idea that they will go through with it "if something more important doesn't come up." And the "something more important" is usually job related, and usually involves value in terms of dollars and cents.

Recognize that leisure time has value too. Not in terms of measurable "dollars and cents," but in terms of long-term effectiveness; in terms of family accord and happiness; in terms of physical health and mental alertness. And in terms of success.

Some of us are guilty of neglecting our home life and giving top priority to our vocation-oriented activities. And we mean well. After all, our career is our bread and butter. It puts food on the table, a roof over our heads, and a car or two in the garage. And the more money we earn, the more tangibles we are able to give to our family and friends — tokens of our love and friendship.

But they're only tokens. If you're interested in giving a costly, yet valuable, gift to someone close to you, consider giving him or her some of your time. It's your most precious possession. You'll be giving them a piece of your life. How could you be more generous than that?

Material gifts are soon forgotten. But the gift of time is never forgotten. It's ironic that some of us spend our time in the pursuit of money and material possessions to give our loved ones. And in so doing, we deprive them of the very thing they want most — our time.

It's too often true that we always have time to attend a friend's funeral, but never had the time to visit him while he was alive.

Surveys have shown that the average work-week of executives is about sixty hours. Lunch hours, evenings, and weekends are used for business-related activities.

Perhaps some executives can put in these kind of hours and still lead a balanced life, but if you're included in this category ask yourself a few questions. Are you forming a work habit that hinders your willingness to delegate to others? Do you find that all this work is leading to exhaustion? Is your retention of information decreased as the work period is increased? Are you depriving yourself of time for self-renewal and creativity? It could be that you are increasing your hours but decreasing your effectiveness.

Don't believe that your income will vary directly with the number of hours you put in. That's a myth. It's what you put into those hours that makes the difference. Get organized and manage your time effectively, and you will accomplish more in eight hours than you did in twelve.

Exhibit 17 shows average distribution of time, assuming a person lives to be seventy years old. Does this approximate the way you spend your time? If so, ask yourself a few questions. Is the results you are achieving by watching T.V. worth eight hours of your life? Are you fully utilizing that six years of travel time? How many of these seventy years include your family? Exhibit 18 shows the same breakdown in a pie chart form. There's not much time left for personal activities when you exclude your career and sleep. How are you spending the precious peice of personal time that's left after the other essentials such as eating, dressing, illness are also excluded? Is the career section expanding to wipe out most of this personal time?

There's only one way of preventing your career from wiping out the rest of your life, and that's by scheduling your meaningful activities into your planning diary and forcing your career to flow around these protected "islands" of time. This is depicted in

Exhibit 19. Put whatever is important to you in the centre of your life and protect it from the demands of your career and other people.

Time is life. Don't waste it on trivial matters. Use it for those priorities that are meaningful to *you.*

Exhibit 17

An average life distribution of time

Sleep	23 yrs.	32.9%
Work	16 yrs.	22.8%
TV	8 yrs.	11.4%
Leisure	4½yrs.	6.5%
Eating	6 yrs.	8.6%
Travel	6 yrs.	8.6%
Illness	4 yrs.	5.7%
Dressing	2 yrs.	2.8%
Religion	½ yr.	0.7%
Total	**70 yrs.**	**100%**

Exhibit 18

Average Life Distribution of Time

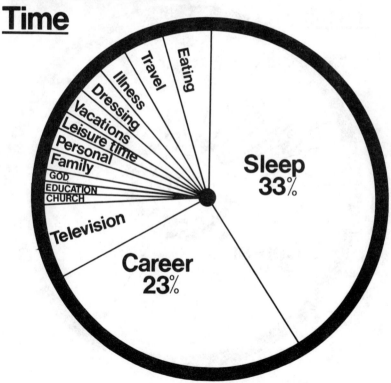

Eating

Travel

Illness

Dressing

Vacations

Leisure time

Personal

Family

GOD

EDUCATION

CHURCH

Television

Sleep
33%

Career
23%

Exhibit 19

Balanced Life Distribution of Time

Other Activities

FAMILY

GOD

FRIENDS

Sleep
About 33%

Career
About 23%

CONCLUSION

Reviewing time management ideas and launching a continuing program of personal organization.

CONCLUSION

Time management is self-management. To get control of your life, you have to first get organized, getting rid of the self-imposed time wasters in your life.

Then you have to reduce the amount of time spent on the time obligations such as correspondence and paperwork. Once you have done this, you will have more time to spend on the priorities — those meaningful activities which will lead you closer to your personal and organizational goals.

In this book I have concentrated on personal organization since it is by far the most important step in getting control of your time and your life. But there are other areas which will require your attention. Read other books on time management and put into practice any ideas which will help you. Naturally, I'm biased when I recommend my previous book, *Making Time Work For You* (General Publishing, 1981), but it's a good place to start.

A bibliography of other time management books is included at the end of this book for your reference. Time management is a never-ending process. You won't become organized overnight. But if you start today by making some of the recommended changes to your personal work habits, and every day make one additional improvement — whether it be a rearranged office, a personal organizer book, or a follow-up file system — you will be organized in the future.

And you know how fast the future closes in on us.

TIME MANAGEMENT BIBLIOGRAPHY

Other books on the topic of time management and self-management for the more avid reader.

TIME MANAGEMENT BIBLIOGRAPHY

Angus, Helen Y. *The Let's Get Organized Workbook.* Toronto: Methuen Publications, 1982.

Bennett, Arnold. *How To Live on Twenty-four Hours a Day.* Garden City, New York: Doubleday & Company, 1910.

Bliss, Edwin. *Getting Things Done.* New York: Charles Scribner's Sons, 1976.

Bond, William J. *1001 Ways To Beat The Time Trap.* New York: Frederick Fell Publishers Inc., 1982.

Cooper, Joseph D. *How To Get More Done In Less Time.* New York: Doubleday & Company, Inc., 1962.

Davidson, Jim. *Effective Time Management: A Practical Workbook.* New York: Human Sciences Press, 1978.

Douglas, Merrill E. and Donna N. Douglass. *Manage Your Time, Manage Your Work, Manage Yourself.* New York: AMACOM, 1980.

Drucker, Peter F. *The Effective Executive.* New York: Harper & Row, 1966.

Ellis, Albert, and William J. Knaus. *Overcoming Procrastination.* New York: New American Library.

Fanning, Tony, and Robbie. *Get It All Done and Still Be Human.* New York: Ballantine Books.

Feldman, Edwin B. *How To Use Your Time To Get Things Done.* New York: Frederick Fell Publishers, Inc., 1970.

Ferner, Jack D. *Successful Time Management.* New York: John Wiley & Sons, 1980.

Goldfein, Donna. *Every Woman's Guide to Time Management.* California: Les Femmes Publishing, 1977.

Januz, Lauren Robert, and Susan K. Jones. *Time Management For Executives.* New York: Charles Scribner's Sons, 1981.

Laird, Dr. Donald A., and Eleanor C. Laird. *The Technique of Getting Things Done.* New York: McGraw Hill, 1947.

Lakein, Alan. *How To Get Control of Your Time and Your Life.* New York: Peter Wyden, Inc., 1973.

Le Boeuf, Michael. *Working Smart: How To Accomplish More in Half the Time.* New York: McGraw-Hill Ryerson, 1979.

Lebov, Myrne. *Practical Tools and Techniques for Managing Time.* New York: Executive Enterprises Publications Co., Inc., 1980.

Lee, John, with Milton Pierce. *Hour Power: How To Have More Time For Work and Play.* Illinois: Dow Jones Irwin, 1980.

Love, Sydney F. *Mastery and Management of Time.* Englewood Cliffs, New Jersey: Prentice-Hall, Inc., 1978.

Mackenzie, Alec, and Kay Cronkite Waldo. *About Time! A Woman's Guide to Time Management.* New York: McGraw Hill, 1981.

Mackenzie, Alec. *The Time Trap.* New York: AMA-COM, 1972.

Marvin, Philip. *Executive Time Management — An AMA Survey Report.* New York: AMACOM, 1980.

Materka, Pat Roessle. *Time In, Time Out, Time Enough.* Englewood Cliffs, New Jersey: Prentice Hall, Inc., 1982.

McCullough, Bonnie Runyan. *Bonnie's Household Organizer.* New York: St. Martin's Press, 1980.

Modern Business Reports. *Getting Control of Your Time.* New York: Alexander Hamilton Institute, Inc., 1978.

Porat, Fireda. *Creative Procrastination.* New York: Harper and Row, 1980.

Rutherford, Robert D. *Administrative Time Power.* Texas: Learning Concepts, Inc., 1978.

Rutherford, Robert D. *Just In Time: Immediate Help for the Time Pressured.* New York: John Wiley and Sons, 1981.

Scott, Dru. *How To Put More Time In Your Life.* Toronto: McClelland and Stewart Ltd., 1980.

Silcox, Diana, with Mary Ellen Moore. *Woman Time.* Wyden Books, 1980.

Stein, Mark L. *The T Factor.* New York: Playboy Paperbacks, 1976.

Steiner, Duane R. *Stretching Time.* Arizona: Deccom, 1982.

Stokes, Stewart L. Jr.. *It's About Time.* Massachusetts: CBI Publishing, 1982.

Taylor, Harold L. *Making Time Work For You: A Guidebook to Effective Time Management.* Toronto: General Publishing, 1981.

Webber, Ross A. *Time Is Money: The Key to Managerial Success.* New York: The Free Press, a division of MacMillan Publishing Co., 1980.

Winston, Stephanie. *Getting Organized.* Warner Books, 1979.

Young, Pam, and Peggy Jones. *Sidetracked Home Executive.* New York: Warner Books, Inc., 1981.

The following time management books are written from a Christian perspective:

Alexander, John W. *Managing Our Work.* Downers Grove, Illinois: Inter-Varsity Press, 1975.

Anson, Elva, and Kathie Liden. *The Compleat Family Book.* Chicago: Moody Press, 1979.

Bowman, George M. *Clock Wise.* Old Tappan, New Jersey: Fleming H. Revell Co., 1979.

Dayton, Edward R., and Ted W. Engstrom. *Strategy for Living.* Glendale, California: Regal Books, Division of G/L Publications, 1979.

Douglass, Stephen B. *Managing Yourself.* San Bernadino, California: Campus Crusade for Christ, 1978.

Engstom, Ted W., and David J. Juroe. *The Work Trap.* Old Tappan, New Jersey: Fleming H. Revell Company, 1979.

Flynn, Leslie B. *It's About Time.* Newton, Pennsylvania: Hearthstone Publications, Inc., 1974.

King, Pat. *How To Have All The Time You Need Every Day.* Wheaton, Illinois: Tyndale House Publishers, Inc., 1980.

Kehl, D.G. *Control Yourself!* Grand Rapids, Michigan: Zondervan, 1982.

Leas, Speed B. *Time Management: A Working Guide for Church Leaders.* Nashville: Abingdon, 1981.

McBride, Pat. *How To Get Your Act Together When Nobody Gave You The Script.* Tennessee: Thomas Nelson Inc., 1982.

Miller, Ruth Wagner. *The Time Minder.* New York: Christian Herald Books, 1980.

Ortlund, Anne. *Disciplines of the Beautiful Women.* Texas: Word, 1977.

Phillips, Mike. *Getting More Done In Less Time and Having More Fun Doing It!* Minnesota: Bethany House Publishers, 1982.

Porter, Mark. *The Time of Your Life.* Wheaton: Victor Books, Division of S. P. Publications Inc., 1983.

Shedd, Charlie W. *Time For All Things.* Nashville, Tennessee: Abingdon Press, 1980.

Whitmore, Nyla Jan. *I Was An Over Committed Christian.* Wheaton, Illinois: Tyndale House Publishers Inc., 1979.

Wiersbe, Warren W. *God Isn't In a Hurry.* Lincoln, Nebraska: Back to the Bible, 1982.

Yohn, Rick. *Getting Control of Your Life.* Nashville, Tennessee: Thomas Nelson Publishers, 1978.

For free information on time management products, literature and seminars available, write to:

Time Management Consultants Inc.
2175 Sheppard Avenue E., Suite 110
Willowdale, Ontario M2J 1W8